# THE SEVEN MOODS OF CRAFT BEER

# THE SEVEN MOODS OF CRAFT BEER

### 350 GREAT CRAFT BEERS FROM AROUND THE WORLD

**ADRIAN TIERNEY-JONES**

BLACK DOG
& LEVENTHAL
PUBLISHERS
NEW YORK

To Jane

Black Dog & Leventhal Publishers
Hachette Book Group
1290 Avenue of the Americas
New York, NY 10104

www.hachettebookgroup.com
www.blackdogandleventhal.com

Originally published in 2017 by Eight Books Limited in
the U.K.
First U.S. Edition: May 2018

Black Dog & Leventhal Publishers is an imprint of
Hachette Books, a division of Hachette Book Group. The
Black Dog & Leventhal Publishers name and logo are
trademarks of Hachette Book Group, Inc.

The publisher is not responsible for websites (or their
content) that are not owned by the publisher.

The Hachette Speakers Bureau provides a wide range of
authors for speaking events. To find out more, go to
www.HachetteSpeakersBureau.com or call (866) 376-6591.

All illustrations by Damian Jaques, Isabel Eeles, and
Lee Martin

Library of Congress Control Number: 2017949737

ISBNs: 978-0-316-51623-5 (flexi-bind);
978-0-316-51622-8 (ebook)

Printed in China

APS

10 9 8 7 6 5 4 3 2 1

# CONTENTS

## INTRODUCTION

# IN THE MOOD
# FOR BEER

**W**hether you want to call it craft, artisanal, independent, or real, the world of beer has never been so exciting, as the traditional countries of brewing (Germany, the Czech Republic, UK, Belgium, the USA) have been joined in the quest for great beer by the likes of Spain, Brazil, and Italy, where brewers are both following global trends and trying to develop styles using raw materials native to their countries.

I am a writer and journalist, a beer-writer if you like, and my day-to-day job involves inspecting and introspecting about beer (as well as drinking it and visiting breweries). Writing this book has been a reminder that my journey is never really over, as I continue on a quest to discover a world of bold-tasting beers from breweries that are encouraging new flavors, rediscovering old flavors, and exciting the palate in the process.

So what have I discovered? First of all, that there are a lot of India Pale Ales (IPAs) being made. This is the beer style that every brewer from Shanghai to Sydney, from Brussels to Portland, Oregon, wants to brew. Little more than thirty years ago, the IPA was an invalid beer style, resting in the wings, slumbering in the armchair of history, the province of no more than a few British brewers, low in alcohol, and, apart from the odd exception, an afterthought. Then came the American beer revolution, in which breweries such as first Sierra Nevada and later the likes of Stone used American hops such as Cascade to revitalize the style, in the process helping to create the American-style IPA (as opposed to the British style). Both now co-exist (in many countries) and have been joined by several variations of the IPA: black, red, Session, Belgian, Imperial, and, more controversial to my mind, tart and fruit IPAs. I recently drank a Raspberry Smoothie IPA — it was interesting and intriguing, but to my mind it was not an IPA; on the other hand, you could argue that beer styles, as in styles of cuisine, music, art, and literature, never stand still, and that the devoted brewer should always be forging ahead.

Let us not forget, though, that other styles are available. There are porters, stouts, golden ales, pale ales, bitters, saisons, and wheat beers (of both the Belgian and the Bavarian traditions); there are beers that have been soured, aged in barrels of various woods, played host to different yeast varieties, and then been blended; and, of course, there is the splendid family of lagered beers, whether they be Pilsners (Bohemian and Bavarian), Dunkels, Viennas, Märzen, or the new kid on the block, the India Pale Lager, or IPL.

One of the more fascinating directions in which the new brewers are taking beer is toward the rediscovery of past traditions. Maybe IPA and porter were the first rediscoveries, but we have also seen the growth of wood-aging and blending, a practice that British brewers in the 19th century were very adept at. Take a look at the brewing books and journals of that century and you will see etchings of the massive wooden tuns that held porter, a dark beer that was aged and blended with a fresher variant. As the 20th century progressed amid world wars, prohibition, changing social patterns, and the emergence of global beer companies, brewers forgot their traditions, the local beers, the quirky beers, the beers that needed time.

Take Leipziger Gose, for instance. I first read of this beer in the pages of one of Michael Jackson's books in the late 1990s and was immediately smitten with the idea of a soured wheat beer that had salt and coriander in the mix. At the time, it seemed like only a couple of breweries were producing one. In 2010, I was in Leipzig on a travel assignment and finally tried one, at Bayerischer Bahnhof, where I spent an afternoon discussing Gose and other beers with the brewmaster, Matthias. How times have changed. Gose is now another fashionable beer style for brewers all over the world. I have had Gose from the USA, the UK, and Italy. Not every one is good, and there is a tendency to flirt with the style and to add all manner of extra ingredients, but the style is saved. On traveling through the pages of the book, you will see evidence of other ancient styles revived: Grodziskie, Adambier, Lichtenhainer, and Berliner Weisse.

All this excitement and exhilaration bode well for the future of beer, although there remain challenges with some countries experiencing high taxation, others having to deal with the insidious rise of what my beer-writing colleague Pete Brown calls "neo-prohibition" — the closure of pubs (a big issue in the UK) — and what some people see as the biggest threat to global independent beer — corporate takeovers. For example, Anheuser-Busch InBev is now responsible for 30% of global beer sales and half the world's profits on beer. Anheuser-Busch has also been very active in buying up craft breweries, especially in the USA, although their modern approach is radically different from the days when such an action would usually have meant closure. We have seen the likes of Goose Island, Camden Town, and Birra Del Borgo go beneath their "Local Champions" wing, while other breweries such as Ballast Point have been bought by other companies. So far, little seems to have changed apart from the beers being more easily found, but this is a future trend that could change and needs to be carefully watched.

The idea for this book came from my wife, Jane. She is not a beer drinker, but we were having a brief discussion on how one could approach a beer book from a totally different angle and out of the blue she said: "the seven moods of beer." The idea developed from there.

Allied with this is that I am often asked what my favorite beer is, and I have long used the stock answer: "It depends on what I am doing at the time." If I want to drink beer in the company of friends, then a brisk bitter or a sprightly Pilsner is more appropriate than an Imperial porter, and so with this in mind I began to develop the idea of suggesting beers that would go with a range of different occasions and frames of mind. This is about beer being flexible, a friend; about something gelling with how the drinkers feel, that might surprise and lead them to surmise how little they knew about the beer in the hand.

I want this book to be a guide that not only charts the global beer revolution but also becomes a companion, that gives drinkers a sense of how important beer can be, a reflection of how they feel when the beer in their hand is drunk and savored.

I hope that you, dear reader and drinker, enjoy it ... and now there is only one thing left for me to ask:

Are you in the mood for a beer? Of course you are.

Adrian Tierney-Jones

# BEER STYLES

**ADAMBIER** — an old German beer style from before the days of the Reinheitsgebot.

**ALT** — amber in color, a hint of citrus, a bitter finish: the beer of Dusseldorf.

**BALTIC PORTER** — a historical remnant of the beers sent to the Russian Empire; dark, full-bodied, creamy, and bittersweet.

**BARLEY WINE** — vinous, fruity, full-bodied, potent; pour one and place yourself in your favorite armchair.

**BELGIAN ALE** — amber colored, with hints of citrus alongside a chewy malt character.

**BELGIAN BLONDE** — honeyed and sweetish with citrus, a creamy mouthfeel and a dry finish.

**BELGIAN STRONG ALE** — whether dark or pale, this is a fruity and boozy beer that is best drunk in small measures.

**BERLINER WEISSE** — tart, acidic, refreshing, brisk in its carbonation.

**BIÈRE DE GARDE** — the classic beer of northern France, which can be gold or amber and has a nutty, chocolaty, praline note mid-palate in between a light oranginess.

**BITTER** — English hops and biscuity maltiness usually produce a potent and boisterous character.

**BOCK** — dark and sweetish, with Doppelbock being its strong and virtuous elder sibling.

**BROWN ALE** — generally sweetish, although American styles have more hop character.

**CHAMPAGNE BEER** — usually strong in alcohol with a Moussec-like mouthfeel, brisk carbonation, gentle citrusiness, and a dry finish.

**CREAM ALE** — light and refreshing, a whisper of malt sweetness.

**DUBBEL** — bittersweet, nutty; dark amber in color, often produced by Trappist breweries.

**DUNKEL** — dark grain, chocolate, and coffee.

**EAST FLANDERS BROWN ALE** — thirst-quenching, bittersweet, slightly tart, clean finish; also known as Oud Bruin.

**FLEMISH RED ALE** — tart, refreshing, lightly acidic, dry finish; historically brewed in West Flanders, Belgium.

**GOLDEN ALE** — lightly malty, gently fruity, finishing bittersweet.

**GOSE** — refreshing, slightly tart, hint of brine, clean finish.

**GRODZISKIE** — light and smoky, refreshing and tart; Lichtenhainer is a close relative.

**GUEUZE** — the champagne of beers; expect a gentle acidity, sharp citrus, and full mouthfeel.

**HEFEWEISSE** — cloves and bananas and brisk carbonation mark out this Bavarian classic as a refreshing if slightly strong (5%+) beer, ideal with food; a hoppier variant is Hopfenweisse, while a stronger version is Weizenbock.

**IMPERIAL STOUT** — strong and seductive, dry and roasty, as strong as a hammer on an anvil; foreign stout is a weaker but still powerful variant.

**IPA** — the beer of the moment, the beer that every brewery makes whether it's American or British style or session, imperial, black, fruit (an abomination in the author's view), tart, or Belgian (look out for Czech, German, and Polish IPAs as well) — oh and let's not forget India Wit Ale and India Pale Lager (or even India Helles Lager).

**KÖLSCH** — delicate beer with a light fruitiness and a dry finish; the beer of Cologne.

**LAMBIC** — tart, grapefruit-like in its fruitiness, fino-like in its dryness; Kriek is a lambic that has been matured with cherries.

**OLD ALE** — dark and malty, usually produced for the winter.

**PALE ALE** — pale, as in veering toward amber at times; American-style pale ales have more grapefruit/citrus character, while British pale ales boast a robust bitterness.

**PILSENER** — Bavarian adaptation of Bohemia's great gift to the beer world, with delicate citrus on the nose and bitterness in the finish.

**PILSNER** — the Ur-lager, the godfather of every blonde lager; Saaz adds floral and spice notes, which are complemented by a bittersweet character.

**PORTER** — the beer of 18th- and 19th-century London; the modern version has a creamy, bitter character.

**QUADRUPEL** — with rich and spirituous, alcoholic and bittersweet love from Belgium.

**RAUCHBIER** — the classic smoked beer of Bamberg, Bavaria.

**SAHTI** — earthy, fruity, slack in its sweetness, a gift from Finland.

**SAISON** — flinty, dry, spicy, and bitter in the finish with a Moussec-like mouthfeel; Wallonia is its homeland.

**SCHWARZBIER** — a refreshing dark lagered beer that is soft and elegant.

**SOUR BEER** — the term can cover a multitude of brewing sins, but the style is a favorite among many craft brewers who look to the traditions of lambic and Berliner Weisse to produce tart, refreshing beers.

**SPÉCIALE BELGE** — amber-colored ale that is dry and bitter with a soft caramel sweetness.

**STOUT** — dry, roasty, and bitter unless it's a creamy Oatmeal Stout or its equally smooth younger sibling, Milk Stout (and not forgetting coffee stout).

**TRIPEL** — a saintly sip first brewed in Belgium; bittersweet and crystalline, honeyed and muscular in its alcohol.

**VIENNA LAGER** — another classic style dating from the 19th century; caramelized malts with a breadiness and sweetness.

**WITBIER** — classic Belgian wheat beer that is spicy and refreshing.

**WOOD-AGED BEER** — beer that has been matured in wooden barrels, which could be sherry, Bourbon, Scotch, or wine.

# HOW TO USE THIS BOOK

MOOD ——————

—————— THEME

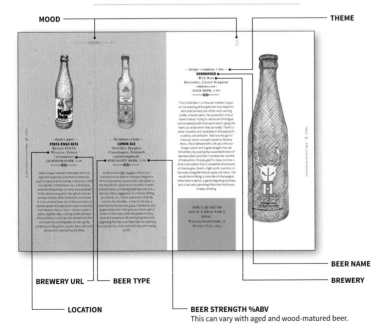

BREWERY URL ——    BEER TYPE ——

—— BEER NAME

—— BREWERY

LOCATION ——

BEER STRENGTH %ABV
This can vary with aged and wood-matured beer.

# BREWERS

## STUART ROSS
Magic Rock Brewing,
Huddersfield, UK

Stuart Ross is a softly spoken Yorkshireman who began brewing in 2004. I met him four years later when he was at a small brewpub in Sheffield, a job that gave him the chance to experiment (smoked Oktoberfest, anyone?). However, it was US beer that crystallized everything for him on being asked to join as head brewer with brothers Richard and Jonny Burhouse when they began Magic Rock in 2011. "The idea," he told me, "was to bring the wonderful fresh flavors of US West Coast IPAs and pale ales to the UK." The result was a range of hop forward and boldly flavored beers.

## YVAN DE BAETS
Brasserie de la Senne,
Brussels, Belgium

Yvan De Baets founded De La Senne with Bernard Leboucq in 2006 and is one of the most articulate and passionate brewers in Belgium. He is an outspoken advocate of bitterness, and often rails against the tide of sweetness that has seemed to sweep through the Belgian brewing scene. It's a good thing he has a superb range of beers to back up his rhetoric, with Taras Boulba, Zinnebir (a Christmas version is often aged and served in the Brussels bar Moeder Lambic), and Jambe de Bois.

# BREWERS

### CHRISTIAN ETTINGER
Hopworks Urban Brewery,
Portland, OR, USA

Before he started Hopworks in 2007,
Christian Ettinger was head brewer at a
neighboring Portland brewery, Laurelwood,
where he brewed two organic beers.
At Hopworks, he has gone the whole gamut,
and all its beers are organic, which he says
is why he is more concerned with the level
of quality of organic raw materials than with
beer styles. Hence, for instance, Survival
Stout, which deviates from the traditional
stout style in its use of ancient grains and
cold-pressed organic coffee.

### ADAM MATUŠKA
Pivovar Matuška, Broumy,
Czech Republic

Even though he's only in his late twenties,
Adam Matuška is one of the most accomplished
figures on the Czech new-wave brewing scene
(mind you, this is no surprise, given that his
father, Martin, is also a well-respected brewer).
As well as top-class pale lagers, he produces
British, American, and German beer styles,
which is perhaps a result of his studies at a
brewing college in Prague, where he was the
first in his class to use dry hopping. Another
feather in his cap was an invitation to judge at
the Great American Beer Festival at the tender
age of 21.

# BREWERS

## TEO MUSSO
### Le Baladin, Piozzo, Italy

"The Jim Morrison of Italian craft brewing," is how one Italian beer writer described Teo Musso, and there is certainly a rock star aura about him, with his tousled hair, trailing multi-colored scarves, and rack-thin figure. However, he's also a towering presence on Italy's beer scene, a creative and restless genius who has overseen the creation of a variety of eclectic beers that were originally influenced by a Belgian brewing mentor and have since gone on their own unique path, using a variety of spices, speciality grains, and different fermentation processes.

## SØREN ERIKSEN
### 8 Wired, Warkworth, New Zealand

Eriksen's beer epiphany came when he was living in Perth, Australia, and he tasted the beers of Little Creatures. Home-brewing followed (not a great success, he has admitted), but then, after moving to New Zealand, he landed a job with Renaissance, where he brewed 8 Wired beers in his spare time. Now he has his own facility where he makes boldly flavored beers that make generous use of New Zealand hops; he is also a big advocate of barrel-aging beers.

# BREWERS

## MARK TRANTER
Burning Sky, Firle, UK

When the affable Tranter founded Burning Sky in 2013, he decided to do things a little bit differently from his former brewery, Dark Star. Yes, he produced an IPA and a pale ale, but what has made him one of the most highly rated brewers in the UK is his fascination with Belgian beer, especially saisons and the wood-aged beers of Flanders. Hence his brewery has its own "barrel farm" in the neighboring barn where a variety of beers slumber until Tranter judges them to be ready.

## JOHN KIMMICH
The Alchemist, Stowe, VT, USA

Kimmich and his wife, Jen, originally started The Alchemist in the town of Waterbury, where it was a brewpub. After 2011's Hurricane Irene destroyed the building, he decided to set up a stand-alone brewery (the couple now have another in Stowe), and made the momentous decision to focus on a single brew, the Imperial IPA cult beer Heady Topper. This was a decision he has never regretted, as he recalled in 2015: "We knew there was nothing like Heady Topper available anywhere around us. So we were pretty confident that we made great beer, and people agreed."

# BREWERS

### DANIEL THIRIEZ
Brasserie Thiriez,
Esquelbecq, France

Thiriez was working in supermarket management when he bailed out and began his own brewery in 1996. He had long nurtured visions of brewing, but he was also in search of the good life: "I wanted to be independent and live in the countryside." Since then, he has made his beers (which are produced in an old village brewery that had previously been closed since 1945) some of the most accomplished on the French craft beer scene, a tribute to his foresight and the risk he took back in the 1990s.

### ERIC TOFT
Private Landbrauerei Schönram,
Petting, Germany

This is a tale of an American going to Bavaria to boss it over a traditional brewery and then turning it into a worldwide star of beer. Toft originally crossed the Atlantic to study brewing, and ended up as the brewmaster in a small village close to the Austrian border. As well as producing a magnificent Pilsner, he was one of the first brewers in Germany to turn his hand to an IPA and an Imperial stout. What makes his achievements all the more remarkable is that he works within the constraints of the Reinheitsgebot, the German beer purity law.

# BREWERS

### BRENDAN VARIS
Feral Brewing, Perth, Australia

Back in 2002 Varis co-founded Feral, about which he has been quoted as saying that he wanted to "craft beers that were a little on the wild side." He is now the sole owner and has been described as the country's first "rock star brewer." Rock star or not, he's certainly been an impressive figure, overseeing the production of award-winning beers such as Watermelon Warhead and Hop Hog, but he is not the kind of brewer to rest on his laurels. For instance, he has conceived a series of sour beers, some of which have been fermented with wild Swan Valley yeasts.

### COSTA NIKIAS
La Sirène, Melbourne, Australia

Wine claimed Nikias first before he turned to beer, an original calling that he readily admits influences La Sirène's focus on French/Belgian-style farmhouse ales. "As an ex-winemaker who used to make Pinot Noir," he told me, "I understand barrels very well, and hence our barrel room that is now 120 strong has many barrel-aged beers fermenting away." This fascination (or could it be obsession?) is also behind him brewing his first 100% spontaneously fermented ale. He says: "Our intention is to focus on wild–fermented beers that reflect our brewery's surroundings and give our products a real sense of place."

THESE ARE BEERS
THAT ARE PLAYFUL,
CELEBRATORY, FRIENDLY, AND
CONVERSATIONAL; BEERS THAT
DESERVE TO BE DRUNK IN THE
COMPANY OF OTHERS TO THE
SOUND OF CLINKING GLASSES
AND SOOTHING VOICES.

# SOCIAL

# UK CITY PUBS

## SMALL BAR
Bristol
{ smallbar.co.uk }

King Street is Bristol's "craft beer quarter," which is where Small Bar (above) is located. It's a high-ceilinged corner bar that isn't that small, as it has an adjoining drinking space as well as a cozy upstairs space. In this case, small refers to the measures offered in the bar, 1/3rds or 2/3rds, but no pints (the Hanging Bat was a pioneer in this). The beer is judiciously chosen, featuring such stars as Siren, Moor, Magic Rock, and the bar's own brewery's Left-Handed Giant.

## TINY REBEL CARDIFF
Cardiff
{ tinyrebel.co.uk }

Another "craft beer quarter," this time centered on Westgate and a tap for award-winning Welsh brewers Tiny Rebel. Naturally it features a boisterous selection of their beers, both in cask and keg, while the decor of a former city center pub is bare wooden floors, steel ducts above the bar, and graffiti on the walls. Think warehouse aesthetic veering toward post-industrial, while you devour the likes of Cwtch or Saaz-succulent Czech-style lager Bo'Ho.

## THE HANGING BAT
Edinburgh
{ thehangingbat.com }
~~~

There's an elemental feel to The Hanging Bat, a mash-up of well-scrubbed wood and bare brick, plus a stainless steel nano-brewery captured behind glass. Scandi-style perhaps, with added beers. People come here to gorge on IPAs, porters, saisons, and beers that defy convention — think the aristocrats of the British beer revolution. And then there's the food — BBQ is the way to go with smoked hot dogs, ribs, and wings. This is a thoroughly modern beer experience.

## CRAFT BEER CO.
London
{ thecraftbeerco.com }
~~~

From the outside, this looks like an old-school boozer standing imperious on the corner of Clerkenwell's lively Leather Lane. Step inside and you're in the midst of a modern craft beer bar, one of several in London opened by the same company. The big open bar is light and luminous, with the kind of glittery air you'd expect in an art gallery; as you sip your beer (there are 16 hand pumps, as well as the same number of keg taps dispensing some of the best beers in the UK and beyond), take a look at the mirrored ceiling with its ornate wood carvings. Fabulous.

## PORT STREET BEER HOUSE
Manchester
{ portstreetbeerhouse.co.uk }
~~~

Manchester's hip Northern Quarter is home to this pioneering craft beer bar, which opened in 2011 and swiftly became a regular stop for those in search of beer heaven. It's easy to walk past; a three-storied brick building with a bar on both floors, with its name on the outside small and unobtrusive. There's cask beer, new-wave keg, and an encyclopedic selection of bottled beers from around the world. Add on events such as "Meet the Brewer" and special beer launches, and you're in nirvana in a city that does beer so well.

## THE SHEFFIELD TAP
Sheffield
{ sheffieldtap.com }
~~~

"The train is now leaving" is not such a disturbing sound if you're standing on Platform 1 at Sheffield Station, because it is here that the Tap is located, a vibrant palace of beer (and a former Edwardian "refreshment room") that was reopened in 2010 after being closed for years. It's plush and understated in the decor (big mirrors, cosy banquettes, a long mahogany bar), while more than 20 cask and keg beers, plus 200 bottles, cater to thirsty travelers eager to sample beers from some of the best breweries in the UK and across the world.

## BLIND TIGER ALE HOUSE
New York, NY
{ blindtigeralehouse.com }

Walk into the Blind Tiger (above) just after opening time and you'll see a row of bar stools at the well-worn wooden bar ready and waiting for the daily influx of regulars and beer tourists. Take one look at the beer selection on the blackboard and you'll see why they come — how about a mug of Bear Republic Prickly Pear Black barrel-aged strong ale, or just take it easy with Left Hand's Milk Stout? The choice is yours.

## THE PINE BOX
Seattle, WA
{ pineboxbar.com }

Once a funeral home, The Pine Box is now a lively craft beer bar with 32 draft beers on tap, alongside a well-chosen bottle range. There's a focus on West Coast breweries such as 21st Amendment, 3 Magnets, Barley Browns, Lagunitas, and Hair of the Dog, alongside the odd US cask beer.

## TORONADO

San Francisco, CA

{ toronado.com }

A visit to San Francisco is incomplete without popping into this down-to-earth (some would say dive-like) boozer in Haight-Ashbury. The beer list features some of the best products of West Coast breweries such as Stone, Avery, and local beer heroes Anchor, whose barley wine Old Foghorn is often on draft.

## MONK'S CAFÉ

Philadelphia, PA

{ monkscafe.com }

Hello Belgium. This Philly institution not only has the look of a bar you might find on a corner in Brussels, but also has perhaps the most extensive Belgian beer list in the United States, both on draft and in bottle (including some rarities). US beers are not forgotten, while the robust dishes feature Belgian classics such as mussels and frites.

## BELMONT STATION

Portland, OR

{ belmont-station.com }

On the corner the bottle shop and bar Belmont Station stands, unassuming and almost diner-like in its appearance. Step inside and there are more than 1,200 bottles of world-class craft beer to choose from, alongside a judicious selection of draft taps. In a city that those in the know call Beervana, Belmont is a shining beacon of beer love.

## FALLING ROCK TAP HOUSE

Denver, CO

{ fallingrocktaphouse.com }

Come the fall, beer-lovers head to Denver, home of the annual Great American Beer Festival. Falling Rock is usually on the itinerary as well, though it's worth visiting at any time of the year. There are usually 70 draft beers to pick from, with the likes of Avery, Stone, Great Divide, and Crooked Stave well represented. The onion rings are pretty awesome as well.

*— Tea for two —*
### MINIMATTA EARL GREY SESSION ALE
Yeastie Boys
Wellington, New Zealand
{ yeastieboys.co.nz }
PALE ALE, 4%

Tea is a sociable drink, as is beer, and the Yeastie Boys had the idiosyncratic idea of merging the two to produce a highly drinkable session beer, a beer–tea ceremony if you like. Drink with the clink of glasses rather than china cups, and enjoy the hints of lemon, bergamot, and ripe peach on the nose, before moving on to a crisp carbonation, light citrus, shades of Earl Grey, and a long dry finish that encourages another sip. Like tea, this is a beer that can be enjoyed at any time of the day, though it's probably at its best in a beery version of afternoon high tea.

*— The plain-spoken pint —*
### MANCHESTER BITTER
Marble Brewing
Manchester, UK
{ marblebeers.com }
BITTER, 4.2%

Straw gold in the glass, pale and thoroughly interesting, this beer booms away with juicy citrus aromatics (oranges and lemons) and a grainy, toasty undertone on the nose, a plain-spoken pint that speaks its mind and has a sense of its own value. "I am what I am," you can almost hear it say as it settles in the glass, with a thick northern-style foamy head suggestive of whipped cream. It is full-bodied, crisp, and appetizing, with a bitterness and dryness resonating all the way through its long finish.

— The beer-garden babbler —

## DOUGALL'S 942

Cerveza Dougall's
Cantabria, Spain
{ dougalls.es }
PALE ALE, 4.2%

————❧————

Bright and colorful in the surge of hop and
fruit aromatics that emerge from the glass, this
zesty, zingy, pale ale is the kind of beer made
for friends gathering together in a beer garden,
happy to see each other, while enjoying the
beer. There's a sweet, friendly, citrusy note on
the nose, alongside a warm-hearted hint of
white grapes, while it's juicy and quenching in
the mouth, with both citrus and tropical fruit
blessing the palate, before the bittersweet
finish. Brewed in the heart of rural Cantabria in
northern Spain, this is a beer that reflects the
sunny, social side of life out there.

"WHEN THE FIRST
ENGLISH ROAD WAS
MADE THE FIRST
ENGLISH INN WAS
BORN."
THOMAS BURKE, 1943

SEVEN MOODS OF CRAFT BEER    SOCIAL

SEVEN MOODS OF CRAFT BEER

*— The garrulous gargler —*

**NECK OIL**

Beavertown

London, UK

{ beavertownbrewery.co.uk }

SESSION IPA, 4.3%

This beer began life as a classic Midlands-style bitter when Beavertown was launched in 2012, apparently based on the beers that brewery founder Logan Plant supped and sought out in the company of mates during his youth. Now it has been re-reformulated as a boldly hopped Session IPA, brimming with a lip-smacking swathe of tropical fruitiness, which is joined and rejuvenated by the firm bitterness in the finish. As the name suggests, this is the kind of beer to drink with friends in a bar while talking about the state of the world.

*— The whisperer —*

**MAZÁK 11° SVĚTLÝ EXTRA HOŘKÝ GALAXY**

Pivovar Mazák

South Moravia,

Czech Republic

{ pivovarmazak.cz }

PILSNER, 4.3%

The gossamer-light touch of dry-hopping with the hop variety Galaxy is evident on both the nose and palate of this lithesome Pilsner-style beer from a brewery in the center of South Moravia. There's a fruitiness, perhaps some peach, a hint of grapefruit, and even a brief breath of mango on the nose, alongside a sweet biscuitiness; meanwhile, the taste is equally fruity, smooth and yet crisp, with a long, winding road of a dry finish. It's the kind of beer that knows how to whisper sweet nothings in the ears of the beer drinker.

*— Iberian eloquence —*

**PALE ALE**

Naparbier

Noáin, Navarre, Spain

{ naparbier.com }

PALE ALE, 4.4%

Pale — as in bruised gold — with glints of sunlight in the glass. Juicy and fruity on both the nose and the palate, as if biting into the flesh of a sensually ripe tropical fruit such as a mango or a papaya; this is then also joined by a passion-fruit lusciousness, which transports you to a vacation in the Pacific. And then, in a microsecond, before this exemplary American pale ale turns into a soft drink lying on a beach, there's a pepperiness in the background and then a bracing dryness that says: "This is a beer, drink deeply of it."

*— The raconteur —*
## HEART & SOUL
Vocation
Hebden Bridge, UK
{ vocationbrewery.com }
SESSION IPA, 4.4%

Gorgeously golden, this Session IPA chirps and chatters away, telling tales of the hops that have come over from the West Coast of America and given it its fresh and fruity character. There's a hint of passion fruit, juicy and lubricious; a suggestion of grapefruit, which brings to mind breakfast; and gooseberry, pineapple, and mango. And if that's not enough, there's a dryness in the finish, alongside an appetizing bitterness. This beer could tell tales all day long.

*— Keep on talking —*
## CROSSBONES
Heavy Seas
Baltimore, MD, USA
{ hsbeer.com }
SESSION IPA, 4.5%

A Session IPA is the kind of beer that gathers people in a group and lets them talk about whatever comes to mind, while the beer adds fuel to the flow of words, though its low alcohol avoids the kind of social immolation that leaves drinkers ruing the following day. With that in mind, CrossBones brings elements of flowery and citrusy notes into the conversation, both on the nose and the palate, all of which are joined by a bittersweet, caramel-like background, and the sort of long, dry finish that would last an ocean crossing.

*— Cold to begin with… —*
## L'AMÈRE DE GLACE
Le Trou du Diable
Quebec, Canada
{ troududiable.com }
PILSNER, 4.5%

Shy and golden when first poured, this well-hopped Pilsner is soon babbling away, telling all and sundry about its crisp freshness, gossamer-light body, delicate fruitiness, and gentle carbonation. It's a fine and noble example of how classic Pilsners have been transformed by craft brewers around the world, without losing the charm and elegance that made them so popular in the first place. Take this to a party, and you'll not be alone. The name of the brewery translates as Devil's Hole, a natural feature of a river that passes through the brewery's hometown.

— *At ease in all situations* —
### LA BLANCHE
Brasserie du Mont
Blanc
La Motte-Servolex,
France
{ brasserie-montblanc.com }
BELGIAN-STYLE
WITBIER, 4.7%

This Belgian-style Witbier
with a French background is
tangy and refreshing, with
a perfect balance of spice
and orange fruitiness on the
palate. The carbonation is
brisk and sprightly, a tingle
on the tongue, a delightful
little prickle that peps up the
palate. There's an elegance
and an understanding about
this award-winning beer,
which makes it very grown up
and happy in all social situations, either as a delicate thirst
quencher or as a
companion on the table to a
ripe blue cheese that spreads
like butter.

— *Sometimes reserved* —
### PO GODZINACH - CHERRY MILK STOUT
Browar Amber
Bielkówko, Poland
{ browar-amber.pl }
MILK STOUT, 4.7%

Milk stout is the English beer
style that hovers on the
margins, a shy and reserved
type uncertain of its status,
overawed by the noise and
poise of the more assertive
members of the stout family.
However, there's a certain
charm about its tranquillity;
it's a self-contained kind of
beer. This Polish take on the
style sees the mocha coffee/
chocolate/creaminess of milk
stout being suffused with
the sour-sweetness of cherry
flavors, and our friend in the
corner is suddenly not so
reserved.

— *Calm and collected* —
### ALL DAY IPA
Founders Brewing
Grand Rapids, MI,
USA
{ foundersbrewing.com }
SESSION IPA, 4.7%

As the name suggests, this
is the kind of beer of which
you can have several without
falling into a stupor, a ringing
endorsement of the
capabilities of one of Michigan's
most highly rated brewers.
It's a fresh-tasting and complex
beer that progresses from
juicy citrus and tropical
fruit on the nose to further
fruitiness on the palate, and
a dry, bittersweet finish. It's
a conversationalist of a beer,
a talker rather than a ranter,
but also calm and collected
and letting everyone around
have their say. We should
have more people and beers
like this.

*— In search of dry wit? —*

## FOURPURE PILS

Fourpure Brewing
London, UK
{ fourpure.com }
HOPPY PILSENER, 4.7%

Another new-wave hop-fused Pils from the London crowd, exemplarily brewed, and one of the first to take up the can and run with it. However, what really stands out about this beer is the Oscar Wilde–like dryness in the finish, which demands the drinker take another sip (or gulp even), and maybe let loose the odd epigram. Elsewhere, it's bruised gold in color, sitting beneath a firm head of rocky foam, with a crisp, snappy, floral nose, while there's a lemony, bittersweet, juicy, lip-smacking lusciousness about the palate. Then it's back to the dry finish once more.

*— The crowd-pleaser —*

## FMB "101" BLONDE ALE

Figueroa Mountain
Brewing, CA, USA
{ figmtnbrew.com }
BLONDE, 4.8%

Sometimes all we want from a beer is something simple yet eloquent, something that says hello and why don't you sit down and have a glass. This honeyed, lightly floral, and crisp Blonde is such a beer, a beer that hangs around in a crowd, shoots the breeze, and tells stories without too much effort. It's a crowd-pleaser, an easy-drinking, quick-thinking, pale gold beer that is refreshing, medium-bodied, and clean on the palate. This is a beer for that social occasion where all is at ease; maybe a day on the beach, or a sundowner on the porch.

*— Dancehall thirst-quencher —*

## RUDEBOY PILSNER

Murray's, Port
Stephens,
NSW, Australia
{ murraysbrewingco.com.au }
PILSNER, 4.8%

The Czech Pilsner style gets an Australian craft makeover with traditional brewing techniques coming up against a hop infusion of New Zealand Motueka and Pacifica. The result is a light and clean-tasting beer with a grainy, biscuity sweetness contrasting with a tropical fruitiness thanks to the hops. It's a beer that is both eloquent and heady in the way it dances on the palate, a sound system of liveliness and a lust for life that make it one of Australia's finest craft lagers. This is definitely a beer to have before and/or after you step out onto the dance floor.

*— The quietly confident one —*

**TZARA**

Thornbridge

Bakewell, UK

{ thornbridgebrewery.co.uk }

KÖLSCH-STYLE ALE, 4.8%

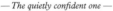

We travel to Cologne by way of Derbyshire for Thornbridge's fresh and willowy take on the classic Kölsch, a beer style that is about being understated and quietly confident in the glass. It's pale gold in color, with a light lemony dusting of sweetness on the nose; there's also a freshness on the nose, almost reminiscent of the ozone-like lightness that emerges from Epsom bath salts. It's light on the palate, with more lemon, a sprightly sense of carbonation, and there's a refreshing, bittersweet finish. This is the kind of beer that starts the evening quietly but, as time passes, tales are told and songs are sung.

*— Alfresco ale —*

**SUN DAZED KÖLSCH-STYLE ALE**

Old Town, Portland, OR, USA

{ otbrewing.com }

KÖLSCH-STYLE ALE, 4.8%

The sun is out, the BBQ is fired up, friends are arriving, and you want to hand out a beer. How about this sunny Kölsch-style ale that is made in Portland, though influenced by the beer that Cologne calls its own? It's fresh and snappy on the palate, crisp and refreshing — just like the cool breeze that has blown through the garden — and, best of all, it's got a dry, bittersweet finish, which is how everyone will feel when the last bottle is emptied.

*— The celebratory pourer —*

**CALYPTRA**

Jack's Abby Brewing

Framingham, MA, USA

{ jacksabbybrewing.com }

SESSION IPL, 4.9%

Jack's Abby co-founder Jack Hendler has always been keen on pushing the boundaries of what is meant by lager — Calyptra is a joyful and melodious example of this colorful approach. Designated as a Session IPL (India Pale Lager), its nose is dominated by a brace of intense hops, Calypso and Citra, with a flurry of citrus and tropical fruit, while one sip brings in more intense fruity notes (think mango, passion fruit, and pineapple, alongside a slap of grapefruit), into which a balance of malt sweetness wraps itself. The finish is appetizingly grainy and dry. This is a beer that hollers its joy of life from the rooftops.

*— An elegant presence —*

**PALE ALE**

Moo Brew

Tasmania, Australia

{ moobrew.com.au }

PALE ALE, 4.9%

There's an elegance about the bottles that Moo Brew use for their well-made beers, an elegance that is adeptly transferred to their beers, such as this aromatic American-style pale ale, whose nose pulsates with pungent aromatic notes of fruit and floral goodness. The palate has an equally smooth fruitiness (think sweet oranges and lemons), alongside a gentle caramel sweetness, and a soft bitterness in the finish. This is not a big barnstormer of a pale ale, trailing pine cones, ripe mangos, and hefty hop sacks in its way, but rather it's elegant (that word again) and subtle, and all the better for it.

*— A discursive beer —*

**NEU BLK**

And Union

Bavaria, Germany

{ andunion.com }

DUNKEL, 5%

Dark amber, burnished chestnut-brown is the color of this unfiltered Dunkel, a beer with a crispness, a briskness, a friskiness, and a complete lack of dissonance, such is the integration of the light chocolate and toffee notes, a hint of fruit, a sprightliness on the palate, and a dry finish that also has a hint of black pepper in the background. It's a beer that wants to talk, that wants to discuss the matters of the world and — such is its color — it would love to be able to do it on a long winter's night, when its amber hue would match the mood of those sitting around the table as the seasons change.

*— A social chameleon —*

**BAMBERG CAMILA CAMILA**

Cervejaria Bamberg

São Paulo, Brazil

{ cervejariabamberg.com.br }

PILSNER, 5%

Czech-style Pilsner can be seen to be a curious kind of beer; it's at once delicate, with its toasted grain nose and light spicy hoppiness, but also assertive, with its bitter dry finish. There's an iron fist in its velvet glove. With this in mind, Camila Camila is a forthright character — the malt gives a sweetness and softness to both nose and palate, and then the Saaz hops start to make themselves known; meanwhile the finish is appetizingly dry. This is a beer ideal for those witty conversations with friends.

SEVEN MOODS OF CRAFT BEER   SOCIAL

— *A bittersweet exile* —
### BOHEMIAN PILSNER
Cervejaria Wäls
Belo Horizonte, Brazil
{ wals.com.br }
PILSNER, 5%

It's a long way from Pilsen to
Brazil, which is perhaps why
this interpretation of a Czech-
style Pilsner has a
bittersweetness about its
nature, a feature that it is
eager to tell all those who
pick up a glass of it about.
The bright gold of its color is
almost like an overkeen suitor
to the biscuity sweetness
and lemoniness on the nose,
an avid flash of memory of
the beer style's birthplace
perhaps. The palate is lemon-
accented, and accompanied
by an undercurrent of herbal
spiciness, but it's the
bittersweetness of the beer in
both mid-palate and on the
finish that tells the true story.

— *The seasonal companion* —
### LITTLE BEER VIENNA
The Little Beer
Corporation
Guildford, UK
{ littlebeer.co.uk }
VIENNA LAGER, 5%

Before there was Pilsner,
there was Vienna lager, a
stopping point on the road to
the Damascus of pale lager,
but this robust, mouth-filling
beer style thankfully never
vanished. This example,
brewed by former corporate
brewing man Jim Taylor,
which also breaks the rules by
using Nelson Sauvin hops, is
pale amber in color, with an
embrace of bready, biscuity,
caramel notes on the nose,
while it's juicy, softly roasty,
and fruity on the palate;
there's also an edge-of-palate
sourness that adds to its
quenching character.

— *Amiable* —
### EPIC LAGER
Epic Brewing
Auckland, New Zealand
{ epicbeer.com }
PREMIUM LAGER, 5%

Hi, I'm a lager, a sociable kind
of beer, the kind of beer that
likes hanging out with others
of a similar disposition,
chatting about this and
that, and keeping drinkers
refreshed. I'm from Auckland
in New Zealand, don't you
know, a cool kind of place, and
just like the city I'm a cool kind
of lager, no frills, no fancies,
just pure refreshment. I'm
crisp, I'm zingy, I've got sweet
citrus and toasted grain on the
nose, nothing too
overwhelming, but
sometimes, just sometimes,
I'm the best kind of beer that
goes with the best kind of
social gatherings.

*— Smooth talker —*

## TIPOPILS

Birrificio Italiano
Lurago Marinone, Italy
{ www.birrificio.it }
**PILSENER, 5.2%**

It's the mid-1990s in Italy, and the beer scene is frothy and frail and dominated by the kind of Blonde lagers that are more about refreshment than flavor. The time is ripe for a change of scenery, and along comes Birrificio Italiano in a small town close to Como, north of Milan (there are others too, including Le Baladin). Avid home-brewer Agostino Arioli is the founder, and one of his first beers is this bright and golden Pilsener, which has gone on to become the flagship beer of the brewery (and perhaps one of the best expressions of a Pilsener in Europe). It's big and bold in both nose and flavor, with a crisp and refreshing mouthfeel; on the palate, it's bitter and aromatic, dry and sprightly, fragrant, resiny, powerful, and punchy. The finish is dry and bitter; this is a beer that can be enjoyed on its own or in the company of a plate of grilled squid. Such is Arioli's devotion to getting the very best hops for Tipopils that he drives over to Bavaria to collect his share personally. Come the spring, there's an extra treat for those who make their way to the brewery tap in Lurago Marinone or visit selected bars in Europe — Tipopils' younger sibling, Extra Hop, is released, and it is not unknown for it to be served with a dried hop cone balanced on the fine elegant foam.

*— A foot-stomper of a pale ale —*

### GUINEU DR. CALYPSO

Ca l'Arenys – Cerveza Guineu
Barcelona, Spain
{ guineubeer.com/en }
PALE ALE, 5.2%

❧

This lively American pale ale, which is produced by a brewery north of Barcelona, has a musicality about its character. For a start, its name is a tribute to a Barcelona ska band that has been going since the late 1980s — Dr. Calypso. The beer is also a foot-stomper, a beer that gets the palate moving with its colorful trio of hops — Galena, Citra, and Simcoe — all American varieties known for the fruitiness and verve they bring to the glass. This is the ideal beer to be drunk while listening to a great dance band.

*— Smooth-talking traditionalist —*

### KOHLENTRIMMER SCHWARZBIER

Buddelship Brauerei
Hamburg, Germany
{ buddelship.de }
SCHWARZBIER, 5.3%

❧

Schwarzbier is one of the classical beer styles of Germany, a dark, roasty, smooth-talking beer whose roots are in the state of Thuringia. Buddelship is on the other side of the country in Hamburg, but that hasn't stopped the brewery taking up the style and producing a highly accomplished and complex version. A flurry of brown sugar and caramel notes emerges from the nose, enticing and catching, alongside hints of signature roastiness and chocolate. When tasted, the beer is subtle but svelte in its roastiness, while joined by a caramel-like sweetness, a medium-bodied feel, soft carbonation, and a bittersweet finish.

— *Come together* —
## PALE ALE
Heidenpeters
Berlin, Germany
{ heidenpeters.de }
PALE ALE, 5.3%

I first came across this joyous
beer at the Markthalle Neun in
the Berlin district of
Kreuzberg, an indoor-
orientated market whose
ambience is relaxed, chatty,
and social, a place where
families, local hipsters, and
tourists come together and
celebrate good food and drink.
Upon first taste, I felt that
the beer had the same feel,
the same unifying force, the
same sense of bringing flavors
together to produce one
holistic whole: there's a
flowery fruitiness on the nose,
suggestive of mangoes and
orange, while taste after taste
reveals a quenching and
tropically fruity palate before
its appetizingly bitter finish.

— *The canned beer debater* —
## MAMA'S LITTLE YELLA
## PILS
Oskar Blues
Longmont, CO, USA
{ oskarblues.com }
PILSNER, 5.3%

Come to Colorado and see
what Oskar Blues get up to
when they want to make a
Pilsner-style beer, gold in
the glass, and in a class of
its own with its crisp bite of
carbonation on the palate, a
wraparound malt sweetness
on both the nose and palate,
and a dry, herbal finish. It's the
perfect Pilsner, even though
it's made in Colorado (as well
as South Carolina, where the
brewery has a second site).
This canned beer — something
the pioneering Oskar Blues
have done since 2002 — is an
ideal companion when drunk
with friends.

"THERE IS NOTHING WHICH HAS
YET BEEN CONTRIVED BY MAN
BY WHICH SO MUCH HAPPINESS
IS PRODUCED AS BY A GOOD
TAVERN OR INN."
SAMUEL JOHNSON, 1776

*— The sunny, optimistic pub friend —*
## CALIFORNIA
Pivovar Matuška
Broumy, Czech Republic
{ pivovarmatuska.cz }
**PALE ALE, 5.3%**

So here we are in a Czech pub in the city of Prague, in the company of like-minded souls, friends that everyone who regularly visits a pub or bar has. Not friends that we went to school with, or worked with, or even got married to, but a special kind of friend. This is a friendship that begins and ends within the boundaries of the pub or bar; a friendship of clinking glasses and wishing each other the best; a friendship of taking swigs of delicious beer (no sips here), exclaiming oohs and aahs of delight, and thinking that the night will never end. This pub, this bunch of people, this happy breed of beer, is the essence of sociability, the creative hub of how beer brings people together. The beer that we are enjoying in this Czech pub is called California, an American-influenced pale ale produced by one of the more vibrant Czech craft breweries, Pivovar Matuška. It's a blond-colored beer that sits beneath a thin collar of snow-white foam, up toward which bubbles ladder through the beer. Like the friendship in the pub, it's not heavy-duty or intense; instead it's uncomplicated in its refreshing qualities, straightforward in its sweetish and juicy counterplay between citrus and soft-toasted graininess on the nose; there's a lightly tart lemon character on the palate, conjoined with more sweetish biscuitiness and a dry and bitter finish that makes the mouth ready for another gulp. Like its namesake state, it's a sunny and optimistic beer, just like the friends in the Czech pub you drink it with.

— *The community beer* —

## SCHÖNRAMER GRÜNHOPFEN PILS

Private Landbrauerei Schönram
Petting, Germany
{ brauerei-schoenram.de }
PILSENER, 5.4%

Beer is an essential part of the social fabric of Bavaria's rural communities, especially during village events where locals gather to celebrate their traditions. A local brewery such as Brauerei Schönram will no doubt have seen its beers served as a backdrop to lively parties throughout the centuries, as it was founded in 1780. That's a lot of festivals and a lot of beer, and you might think that such a sense of tradition had stifled the brewery's ambitions.

However, this passage of time has not diminished the brewery's independence and commitment to making great beer, as anyone who has tasted the products that American-born Eric Toft has overseen since arriving as brewmaster in the late 1990s would testify. Grünhopfen Pils is a point of greatness to consider: a ray of golden sun in the glass, topped with a brittle, pure-white collar of foam. There are subtle wafts of light lemon, grassiness, and gently toasted grain on the nose, but it's when you take your first gulp of this wonderful Pils made with fresh green hops that you can understand the emotions and social interactions that come through beer. There's a soft bitterness, a cheer of lemon at the front of the mouth, an elegant and restrained note, while the carbonation cuts at will, parries and thrusts. In the finish, dryness takes hold alongside an herbal note and some fruitiness, and before you know it you're wanting to move to the brewery's home village.

*— Contentment —*
## A MODO MIO PILS
Birrificio San Giovanni
Roseto degli Abruzzi, Italy
{ birrificiosangiovanni.it }
PILSNER, 5.5%

The sigh of contentment with the first sip — or should that be slurp, given the thirst that this lightly golden and delicately floral Pilsner evokes and then provokes? — the nod of the head to the friend opposite, the words of praise evoked . . . This Italian Pilsner is the kind of beer that should always be drunk in the company of others. It is crisp and lightly citrusy on the palate, before it descends into a dry and bittersweet finish that calls once more for another slurp.

*— The talk talker —*
## PILS
Three Boys Brewery
Christchurch, New Zealand
{ threeboysbrewery.co.nz }
PILSNER, 5.5%

You could argue that Three Boys has its background in the social world of English pub land, as the brewery's founder came over from New Zealand to study and then spent five years working in Sheffield, which has claimed to be the beer capital of the UK. Pils was the debut beer, and has remained a bestseller ever since the brewery's foundation in 2004. It has a fresh, ozone-like nose, while, once tasted, it's hard not to fall for its combination of toasted grain and fruit, alongside a spritziness, dryness, and beguiling bittersweetness.

*— Outgoing and gregarious —*

## PUNK IPA

BrewDog
Ellon, UK
{ brewdog.com }
IPA, 5.6%

This is the beer that Scotland's self-proclaimed "punk" brewers announced themselves with: a beer with such a big hit of hops that, unless you saw the label pronouncing the origin as Scotland, you would have sworn that it came from the west coast of the United States. It was loud and noisy, sending hop-fueled fireworks into the calm skies of the UK beer scene from 2007 onward; very quickly it became the brewery's standard-bearer, its punk peacock, its mouthpiece, its voice, its legend. The recipe has been refined since (it was originally 6%), but it's still a big beast of a beer, with a pungent and arousing nose of ripe peach and apricot skin, while lychee, papaya, and mango trip off the tongue, followed by a gentle touch on the elbow of white pepper in the dry and grainy finish. This is a beer that is the perfect accompaniment to every social gathering, a companion and a custodian of craft beer's infernal values, a joy-rider, an outrider, a practitioner of megaphone diplomacy, whose growing age has not slowed it down. Some might find it a beer that never shuts up, but on its arrival there were things that needed saying about British beer, and Punk IPA was the perfect soapbox hero for this.

— *Self-confident and assured* —
## FOUNDATION 11
CREW Republic Brewery
Munich, Germany
{ crewrepublic.de }
PALE ALE, 5.6%

Munich — home of the Oktoberfest, lederhosen, and dirndls; of Helles and Pilsener; the beer gardens where drinkers gather and express their delight at sparkling golden goblets of sunlight. Munich — also home to Foundation 11, a self-confident, self-declared German pale ale, a sign of how the German/Bavarian beer scene has developed. This is an assured and self-confident beer, whose makers have mixed in both Bavarian and American hops, plus malted barleys from Bavaria and England. The result is a shimmering, amber-colored beer with wafts of citrus and berries on the nose, a grainy toastiness alongside further citrus on the palate before its bitter herbal finish. *Gemütlichkeit*!

— *The beach party beer* —
## WINSTON
Shenanigans Brewing
Sydney, Australia
{ shenanigansbrewing.com }
PALE ALE, 5.6%

The idea of sitting on the beach is never far from Sydneysiders' thoughts, especially in the company of a cold and refreshing beer. Instead of the generic Arctic-cold lager, Shenanigans' American pale ale Winston is just the kind of beer to take down to the beach. With an ANZAC-style collaboration of Australian and New Zealand hops providing a fragrant fruitiness on the nose, there is an equal contribution of fruit on the palate before its lip-smacking, bittersweet finish. Ideal for refreshment after trying to better your best mate on his or her board, or for lounging about on the golden sands of Bondi Beach just watching the world go by.

*— The tall-tale teller —*

## CUCAPÁ CHUPACABRAS PALE ALE

Cervecería de Baja
California
Mexicali, Mexico
PALE ALE, 5.8%

In Puerto Rico in 1995, it was reported that a strange, possibly extraterrestrial creature was preying on farm animals; further sightings occurred throughout the Americas. It was nicknamed "Chupacabras," which translated as "goat-sucker," the name that Cucapá gave to this luscious, amber-colored pale ale. Thankfully, there is no horror involved here, instead just the thrill of citrus on the nose and palate, accompanied by hints of caramel sweetness, finishing dry and bitter. As for the Chupacabras — it's now believed to be an urban myth.

*— The fast talker —*

## C5 SAGA ALE BLANCA

Cervecería Cinco de
Mayo
Atlixco, Mexico
{ cc5.mx }
BELGIAN-STYLE
WITBIER, 6%

The brewery claims this to be a Belgian-style ale, but once tasted it's more akin to a Witbier, given the coriander spice and pepperiness on the nose, accompanied by a fresh spritziness. A sip unveils a juicy orangeness, an edge-of-palate sourness, white pepper, a full mouthfeel, and a dry and juicy finish. The sourness somehow brings out the juiciness, making this beer a gulper. Belgian Witbier seems to have been ignored in this hopocalyptic time, but it's a beautiful Belgian style that this Mexican brewery has captured the very essence of.

*— The partygoer —*

## STONE PALE ALE 2.0

Stone Brewing
Escondido, CA, USA
{ stonebrewing.com }
PALE ALE, 6%

Stone Pale Ale was the brewery's calling card to the rest of the beer world when first brewed in 1996 — a highly hopped creation that would take its place in the pantheon of West Coast pales. In 2015, perhaps in celebration of 19 years of fun, 2.0 was unveiled, this time hopped with the German hop Mandarina Bavaria, a bright and bold variety that gives the beer peachy and orangey aromatics and flavors alongside the crisp, biscuity, malt backbone. It's a vividly flavored beer, and well worth a toast at the next party you take it to.

— *The conversationalist* —
### ROWING JACK
AleBrowar
(brewed at Browar Gościszewo)
Lebork, Poland
{ alebrowar.pl }
IPA, 6.2%

"Hop heads of Poland" declaims a slogan adopted by this gypsy brewery, and with Rowing Jack they might have a point. For when hop heads get together they like nothing better than to chat about those beers where *Humulus lupulus* (the common hop) is king. Further food for thought might also be AleBrowar's position as one of Poland's pioneers in the craft beer revolution, plus its gypsy status (many of its beers are brewed at Browar Gościszewo). This beer is the brewery's take on a West Coast IPA. It ululates with tropical fruit notes, calms down with sweet caramel, then returns to tropical fruit and pine before a bracing bitter finish.

— *The pub celebrated in Italian style* —
### REALE
Birra Del Borgo
Borgorose, Italy
{ birradelborgo.it }
IPA, 6.4%

Birra Del Borgo is one of the leading lights of the Italian craft beer movement (which led to it being bought by Anheuser-Busch in 2016, and made some stop drinking its products, such is the fierce partisan support beer engenders). It is noted for experimental beers, such as a tobacco-flavored porter and a terracotta-aged beer, as well as hop-gods such as My Antonia. However, with ReAle we are in the classic confines of the English pub, socializing and spending time with like-minded souls. This beer is a tribute to the English IPA, and has a blast of citrus on the nose, accompanied by peppery hops, and a crisp mouthfeel with plenty of citrus before the lingering bitter finish.

## LITTLE CREATURES IPA
Little Creatures
Brewing
Fremantle, Australia
{ littlecreatures.com.au }
IPA, 6.4%

What do we want the beer to do when we drink it? When a glass of this amber-gold, citrusy, caramel-sweet IPA is poured, maybe the only message we will get is "Drink me," a command that is easily obeyed. This IPA, produced by a brewery best known for its bright summer's day of a pale ale, is equally sunny, with breakfast grapefruit and earthy hop on the nose, grapefruit and passion fruit on the palate alongside a delicate sweetness before a rounded, crispy bitterness that encourages you to start all over again. Sometimes it's enough just to have a conversation with the beer in your glass.

— *The poetry reading* —
### HOPFELIA
Foglie d'Erbe
Forni di Sopra, Italy
{ birrificiofogliederba.it }
IPA, 6.4%

Foglie d'Erbe, the brewery's name, translates as 'Leaves of Grass,' which takes us straight to Walt Whitman's classic collection of humanistic and individual meditations. This is a beer for a poetry reading, perhaps? So while Whitman is being read aloud to the room, the beer complements the words with its light fruity aromatics (melon, mango, passion fruit, pineapple) followed by a gentle bitterness, tropical fruitiness, and bittersweet finish. Like a poem you've read aloud to a loved one, HOPFelia demonstrates the depth and desire of the modern IPA.

43

"TWO INCHES TO THE NORTH-WEST IS WRITTEN A WORD FULL OF MEANING — THE MOST PURPOSEFUL WORD THAT CAN BE WRITTEN ON A MAP. 'INN.'"
A. A. MILNE, EARLY 20TH CENTURY

— *Cheers to this beer* —
## VIVAT BLONDE
Brasserie de l'Abbaye du Cateau
Le Cateau-Cambrésis, France
{ brasserieducateau.fr }
BIÈRE DE GARDE, 6.5%

Each time you order a glass of this smooth and aromatic new school bière de garde there's an affirmation in your voice that greets all those you're drinking with — "*Vivat*" is a version of "Cheers" in the dialect of the part of northern France where Brasserie de l'Abbaye du Cateau started brewing in 2003. There's further evidence of the social and generous nature of the beer in that it's brewed in a former Benedictine abbey, which housed a brewery until 1926, indicating that the monks knew something about raising a toast. Blond in color, the beer has a peppery and citrusy swirl of aromatics with a citrusy, bittersweet palate that finishes dry. Vivat: a cheering beer indeed.

— *Sociability in the heart of sociability* —
## IPA
Brouwerij de Prael
Amsterdam, Netherlands
{ deprael.nl }
IPA, 6.5%

Every one of de Prael's beers is brewed in the midst of one of the most sociable parts of Amsterdam: the Red Light District. Gawkers come and go, while the women parade; tourists with other matters on their minds pass with an occasional shamefaced glance; kids on their way to school and elderly men and women who have lived in the area all of their lives look elsewhere. You could choose any of the brewery's beers as an example of the area's sociability (with the heartening add-on of the company policy to employ people who have struggled with employment due to disability and other factors), but it's the IPA that matches the buzziness of its home area. It has a leafy hoppiness on the nose, grassy even with some grapefruit, while on the palate it is citrusy and bittersweet in the finish. Perfectly sociable.

— *Old friends* —
### RED RACER IPA
Central City Brewers +
Distillers
Surrey, Canada
{ centralcitybrewing.com }
IPA, 6.5%

In some social situations,
maybe three old friends
together, a bit older and wiser,
more sensible when it comes
to having a glass of beer, this
is the sort of IPA that will make
the evening (or it might be an
afternoon in a beer garden)
pass with a warmth and a
mellowness that other beers
won't evoke. There's a blast
of fresh rich citrus on the nose,
plus pine, followed by more
fruit, pine, and a delicate malt
sweetness before the rousing
chorus of dryness and
bitterness in the finish. Glad to
see you again, old buddy.

— *Confound the magician* —
### INDIGO IPA
Deck & Donohue,
Paris, France
{ deck-donohue.com }
IPA, 6.5%

Imagine you are watching a
magician. Somehow you've
been selected to be the guinea
pig. "Pick a color, any color,"
comes the command. You say
indigo, just to be different. The
same train of thought resulted
in this Parisian IPA, whose US
brewers named it as a way
of getting French drinkers to
think differently (blond and
amber seemed to be their own
true colors). With a classic
citrus boost on the nose,
tropical fruit and
earthiness on the palate, and a
dry bitterness lasting forever,
Deck & Donohue have the
crowd on their side.

— *Traveling companion* —
### CLOCK NO IDOLS!
### 15° RYE IPA
Řemeslný pivovar
CLOCK,
Potštejn, Czech
Republic
{ pivovarclock.cz }
RYE IPA, 6.5%

Rye IPA? Think of the bold and
bright colors of an American
IPA (tropical fruits sitting in
a bowl ripened by the sun, a
pine forest after rain, biscuity
sweetness) joined by the
caraway-like spice and pizzazz
of rye and you're getting there.
This piquant shot of hop love
is a seasonal beer that
encourages friends to travel
all the way to the Bohemian
town of Potštejn, where the
relatively young Řemeslný
pivovar CLOCK (it only opened
in 2014) has its small brewing
kit and a bar where you can sit
and taste all day long.

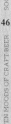

*— The smooth operator —*

### MODUS HOPERANDI

Ska Brewing

Durango, CO, USA

{ skabrewing.com }

IPA, 6.8%

Given the name of the brewery, this is the kind of beer that you would want to keep company with after a good old session on the dance floor, where the ska sounds seemed to go on forever. It's an IPA, of course, skillful and sinful in the way the hops clatter and clang along on the palate, resiny, citrusy, piny, though accompanied by the counterpoint of a bracing malt background. It's rock-steady in its appeal, complex in its call to the palate, while the joyous bitter finish is delightfully smooth, just like the moves you've been making on the dance floor.

*— The exuberant one —*

### FUNKY BUDDHA HOP GUN

Funky Buddha

Oakland Park, FL, USA

{ funkybuddhabrewery. com }

IPA, 7%

The aromatics of the American hops used in this bold and vividly flavored IPA leap out of the glass with the aplomb of an acrobat: ripe grapefruit peel, freshly cut pineapple, and the smell of a forest of pine trees after a sharp shower of spring rain. It's a brooding gold in the glass, with plenty of tropical and citrus fruit and more pine on the palate, accompanied by a caramel smoothness that keeps all this happy and hoppy exuberance in check.

*— The chill-out zoner —*

### NOMÁD KAREL ESKÁ IPA

Pivovar Nomád

Prague, Czech Republic

{ pivovar-nomad.cz }

IPA, 7.6%

This assertively bitter IPA is uniquely hopped with Czech varieties rather than American, which have become the norm for most craft breweries' IPAs. Dark orange in color, it is reflective and relaxed beneath its off-white summit of foam. Aromatic notes of grapefruit, mandarin, and pine quiver on the nose, while the palate is a bittersweet construction of more citrus, a grainy dryness, the whisper of fresh-cut grass, and an appetizing juiciness at the middle of the palate. The finish is dry, and carries further bitter notes that eventually fade away, leaving the memory of a great beer.

— *The brewpub standard* —
### GREEN ELEPHANT
Laurelwood Public
House & Brewery
Portland, OR, USA
{ laurelwoodbrewpub.com }
IPA, 6.9%

Laurelwood makes its beers in
Portland, Oregon, one of the
best beer cities in the world;
it is also a friendly and social
city where brewpubs loiter
on every corner. Laurelwood
is one of these brewpubs, a
place where drinkers drink
deeply of Green Elephant,
Laurelwood's exemplary IPA.
It's bright orange in color, the
start of the sun setting over
the Willamette River perhaps,
then there's a leafy, grassy,
and musky nose, while on the
palate it's dry and tropically
fruity, bursting with pine and
caramel before a long and
friendly bitter finish.

— *Come and have another* —
### ANOSTEKÉ BLONDE
Brasserie du Pays
Flamand
Blaringhem, France
{ brasseriedupays
flamand.com }
BLONDE, 8%

Let's get the meaning of the
name out of the way first.
"*Anosteké*" is Flemish pub slang
for "To the next one," which
is a cheery sentiment readily
understood after one sip of
this fine beer. Yes, it's blond
in color, while fine threads of
bubbles rise to be engulfed by
the fine white mousse of foam.
There is plenty of citrus fruit,
and even a touch of peach skin
on the nose, which gives it a
soft, approachable start. The
palate is bittersweet, citrusy,
herbal, and medium-bodied,
while the finish has a pleasing
bitter finish. Here's to the next
one indeed.

— *Fresh and frisky* —
### BLING BLING
Bridge Road Brewers
Beechworth, Australia
{ bridgeroadbrewers.com.au }
DOUBLE IPA, 8.5%

Drink this beer when it's fresh
and full of deep and booming
fruity hop notes on the nose,
while pine-like, resinous tones
coat the tongue alongside a
voluble babble of bright orange
sweetness and tropical fruit
friskiness. It's hoppy (and how!),
but there's also a fluidity about
this recourse to hoppiness that
makes it more than a one-note
beer difficult to converse with.
As for the name Bling Bling?
This is simply the stronger
sibling of the brewery's equally
delicious IPA Bling.

SOMETIMES AN ADVENTURE IS ABOUT
SEEING HOW FAR A BREWER CAN TAKE
A BEER: BE IT RESURRECTING AN OLD
BEER STYLE OR BREWING A BEER STYLE
ASSOCIATED WITH ONE PLACE IN A
TOTALLY DIFFERENT COUNTRY. POUR
YOURSELF A GLASS AND PREPARE TO
FOLLOW THESE BEERS' ADVENTURES.

**ADVENTUROUS**

# GERMAN PUBS

## SCHLENKERLA
Bamberg
{ schlenkerla.de }

Anyone who is interested in beer should visit Bamberg at least once in their lifetime to sample the incredible beers brewed there in a selection of traditional bars. This homely hideout (above) is where deep draughts of the eponymous classic Rauchbier can be devoured and contemplated. Alongside two rooms (one of which is a locals' favorite) there are nooks and crannies, and in the summer the beer garden is heavenly.

## ZUM UERIGE
Düsseldorf
{ uerige.de }

This is one of four brewpubs in the old center of Düsseldorf that brew the traditional local beer Alt. Inside, "*Kobes*" (as the waiters are known) rove about the multi-roomed establishment, trays filled with glasses of the delicious amber-colored beer. It's a cozy place, where people sit and drink at old wooden barrels, while some rooms have absurdist-style figures painted on the walls. At the back of the pub stands the well-burnished brewing copper.

## BRAUEREI ESCHENBRÄU
Berlin
{ eschenbraeu.de }

This popular brewpub hides itself away off a street in Berlin's Wedding district. Inside there are several rooms, but when the weather is clement drinkers sit in a beer garden shaded with trees and edged in by apartment buildings whose walls are covered in creepers. On the beer card there are well-made classics such as Pilsener and Dunkel, and monthly specialities such as a Schwarzbier, Weizen Doppelbock, and stout. The equally unmissable brewpub Vagabund (vagabundbrauerei.com) is a five-minute stroll away, where Anglo-American influences bring forth the likes of a Szechuan Saison and a Double IPA.

## AUGUSTINER BIERHALLE AND RESTAURANT
Munich
{ augustiner-restaurant.com }

For a classic Munich beer hall experience, this is a good choice. Even though it gets busy, it doesn't have the boisterous bonhomie of Hofbräuhaus. Sets of antlers and dark wood panels line the walls, the wooden tables are scrubbed to within an inch of their lives, and the waiting staff weave about holding trays of gleaming and golden Augustiner Helles, perhaps one of the best expressions of this beer in the world. For a more craft-centric experience, visit Tap-House Munich (tap-house.de).

## BRAUSTELLE
Cologne
{ braustelle.com }

Even though Cologne is noted for its Kölsch beer, with many pubs offering this world classic, this cozy pub is slightly different in that it is the home of small brewery Braustelle, whose kit can be seen at the back of the establishment. Their beers are available on draft, including a red ale, pale ale, and Pink Panther, which is a beer brewed with hibiscus flowers. They also produce their own version of a Kölsch.

## GASTHAUS UND GOSEBRAUEREI BAYERISCHER BAHNHOF
Leipzig
{ bayerischer-bahnhof.de }

This traditional-looking brewpub and restaurant is located in an old railway station. Inside there's lots of dark wood, but the gleam of stainless steel brewing above the main bar is the main reason for a visit. This is one of the few places where traditional Leipziger Gose (unlike those infused with fruit or dark malt) is brewed, and you can drink it here with gusto, as well as a Pils, Schwarzbier, Porter, and occasional specials. For instance, brewmaster Matthias once made a Berliner Weiss with Brettanomyces.

# FRENCH BARS

## LES BERTHOM
Strasbourg
{ lesberthom.com }

Even though we're in France, the city of
Strasbourg is more beer than wine, a situation
that is reflected in the popularity of this busy
and buzzy bar (above) that attracts a young
and lively crowd (it's part of a chain of similarly
beer-centric places in cities such as Lyon, Dijon,
and Le Havre). Around half a dozen beers are
served on tap, while the bottle selection num-
bers about 40 different beers, which come from
all over the world, though there is an emphasis
on the products of Belgium.

## LES TROIS 8
Paris
{ lestrois8.fr }

Here is another sign that Paris is finally joining
the beer revolution that has been sweeping
the world. With eight beers on tap (and they
are consistently rotated), and more than 100
in bottles, this is a place to discover some of
the stars of French craft brewing such as local
heroes Deck & Donohue and Brasserie de la
Goutte d'Or, as well as the likes of Normandy's
Ferme-Brasserie la Chapelle. No meals, but if
you're hungry the bar has a good selection
of charcuterie.

## LA FINE MOUSSE
Paris
{ lafinemousse.fr }

The romantically melancholic cemetery of Père Lachaise is a short stroll from this cozy bar, which is a fine place to enjoy a beer or two after a reflective walk among the gravestones. Inside it's post-industrially modernist, with bare brick walls and a gleaming array of 20 draft taps (there are also more than 100 different bottled beers). French craft beers stand side by side with products from Belgium, the UK, and the United States. There are regular tap takeovers, and the bar has a restaurant opposite.

## COULEURS DE BIÈRES
Montpellier
{ facebook.com/Couleurs-de-Bi%C3%A8res-Officiel-175497609144290 }

Look beyond the bar, and there a black chalk-board skulks, featuring the names of four breweries, their beers, strengths, and styles. Even though there are only four beers featured on tap at any one time, this is a place to check out the French beer scene in the southwest of the country. You might find an Apricot Wit, perhaps, from local brewery Le Détour, or an IPA from Garrigues, which is based in the Languedoc. There is also a sizeable selection of bottles (800!), which is just as well since Couleurs also allows you to buy and take beers home with you.

## LES FLEURS DU MALT
Lyon
{ lesfleursdumaltlebar.fr }

There's plenty of good wine in Lyon, but this basement bar is the place to dive into if you're in search of great beer. Once inside, note the arched ceiling that imbues the surroundings with a sense of contemplation, but then have a look around and the fittings are pure minimalist modernism. The beers? Expect to inspect 300 bottles and 16 draft beers from all over the world, with the likes of De Molen, Mikkeller, and BrewDog (as well as French selections) on offer.

## LA CAPSULE
Lille
{ facebook.com/La-Capsule-120976054751869 }

Compact bar in the old part of Lille that attracts drinkers in search of indie French beers from the likes of Thiriez, St-Sylvestre, and Mont Salève, as well as Belgian classics such as Rodenbach, Dupont, and De Struise — there are usually up to 24 taps dispensing beer, so there's plenty to drink. Stools standing at the bar in the manner of an English pub, a buzzy vibe from the youngish crowd, and cold meats and cheese all add to the attraction.

# BELGIAN BARS

## WATERHUIS AAN DE BIERKANT
Ghent
{ waterhuisaandebierkant.be/waterhuis-prijslijst }

Settle yourself within this cozy, candle-lit old bar, or take a seat on the riverside terrace where you can look out over the Leie and marvel at the surrounding architecture and that you're in one of the best beer bars in Ghent (above). There are more than 150 beers to try, including a couple that have been brewed especially for the bar. There's also room upstairs when, invariably, the place gets busy (the local puppet theater people also rock up there now and again).

## MOEDER LAMBIC FONTAINAS
Brussels
{ moederlambic.com }

This is a classy modern beer bar whose decor is exposed brick walls, big wide windows, a long straight bar, and solid wooden tables standing in serried rows. An enviable selection of beers, both draft and in bottle, will come from Belgian beer heroes such as De La Senne, Val-Dieu, De Ranke, Tilquin, and Cantillon, as well as international classics from Italy, Switzerland, Spain, and the United States. Food is simple but delicious, including quiche, cold meats, and cheese. An essential stop when visiting Brussels.

## BILLIE'S BIER KAFÉTARIA
Antwerp
{ facebook.com/billiesbierkafetaria }

On entering this engaging beer café, visitors are usually scrutinized by Billie the French bulldog, who has given his name to this compact street corner "brown bar," which, even though it only opened in 2013, has quickly become one of Antwerp's top beer destinations. The 100-beer list (both draft and bottle) combines established favorites such as St. Bernardus Abt 12 and Rodenbach Grand Cru alongside newer offerings from Troubador (Triple Spiked Brett, anyone?) and De La Senne. A robust Flemish stew is among a selection of dishes to keep hunger at bay.

## LE POECHENELLEKELDER
Brussels
{ www.poechenellekelder.be }

This vibrant bar directly opposite the Manneken Pis features a list of more than 100 bottled beers, including a small but venerable selection of aged ones. The decor is busy, quirky, and eye-catching: look out for puppets hanging from the walls, a rash of framed pictures and photos, and a selection of beer books in the downstairs bar. It might stand right in the middle of Brussels' city center, where the tourists all too often rush along from sight to sight, but it has a heart and soul that will make you want to linger.

## 'T BRUGS BEERTJE
Bruges
{ www.brugsbeertje.be }

After admiring Bruges' pleasing patchwork of narrow streets and silvery canals, it's time for a beer and 't Brugs Beertje is a classic place to take a pew and a pint. This cozy beer café offers a glass-shattering list of 300 beers (plus snacks), and is visited by beer-lovers from all over the world. Glasses and tankards hang above the bar, and there's often light classical music in the background, but the main soundtrack is one of voices as appreciative drinkers do what drinkers do in pubs: talk and drink beer.

## L'AROMA HOPS
Mons
{ facebook.com/AromaHops }

Post-industrial is the vibe at this city center bar, which opened in 2015 and has rapidly become the Mons beer place to hang out. Light fittings hang like tears and bottles gleam radiantly in fridges behind the bar, while well-polished taps dispense a succulent selection of both classics and new-wave heroes from Belgium and the world. The atmosphere is buzzy and lively, and the place can get packed, but it's a welcome addition to the city's beer scene.

# AUSTRALIAN BARS

## WHEATSHEAF HOTEL
Adelaide
{ wheatsheafhotel.com.au }

On a street corner in the western part of
Adelaide (Thebarton) the Wheatsheaf stands,
looking for all the world like a pub out of early
20th-century Australia; a very ordinary local
watering hole you might think. However, once
inside, expectations change as you scan the list
of exceptional beers from Australia and across
the world — there a beer from Bridge Road,
here one from Stone, and let's not forget the
beers that have been produced by the Wheaty
Brewing Corps since 2014. Sometimes
appearances can be deceptive.

## THE SCRATCH
Brisbane
{ scratchbar.com }

Lively Park Road is the home of this small,
unpretentious bar that stands in the shadow
of a major corporate brewery. Step inside and
forget that bland beers exist, as you are brought
face to face with a beautiful selection of beers
from the likes of Hargreaves, Newstead, and
Brewtale; meanwhile, the bottle collection
will include IPAs, pale ales, wheat beers, and
saisons from Two Metre Tall, Pirate Life, and
Stone. In you go.

## THE GREAT HALL
Fremantle
{ littlecreatures.com.au }

This used to be a crocodile farm, but the snap-
pers are long gone, and instead you can now
enjoy the beers of Little Creatures, which are
brewed onsite (one of two places where these
Australian craft beer pioneers make their beer).
Hall is the right word, with a high ceiling and
luminous sense of light, a lot of it reflecting off
the gleaming brewing kit, which also sits in the
space. Grab a Pale Ale, or maybe Rogers' Amber
Ale, and you're set for a good time.

## DUTCH TRADING CO.
Perth
{ thedutchtradingco.com.au }

Beer? You got it, and a lot of it, at this light and
airy bar that opened in Victoria Park in 2015.
There are 18 taps, with beers from the likes of
Lucky Bay, Boatrocker, and Bootleg, as well as
Sierra Nevada, Mikkeller, and Nøgne ø — there
is also a selection of 300 bottles, so no one need
go thirsty. And the name? It's something to do
with the Dutch love of exploration several
centuries ago, which manifests itself in the way
this exemplary bar explores the world of beer.

## PREACHERS BAR
Hobart
{ facebook.com/pg/preachershobart }

A former church? Afraid not: this cozy craft beer bar was once a curry house, but there's still an element of righteousness in the way some of the best Tasmanian indie beers are served up with joy and abandonment in an atmosphere that some say reminds them of an English country pub. It's hip and holistic in the way good beer is celebrated. How about a glass of Two Metre Tall's Forester Ale, or maybe something from Mountain Goat?

## BITTER PHEW
Sydney
{ bitterphew.com }

Just off Sydney's lively and colorful Oxford Street, this small bar (above) is a quiet and reflective place that majors in some of the best beers it can find (as well as whiskies and ciders) — there are 12 taps and a large bottle selection so, once you're in, expect to stay for a while. It's cozy and contemplative, and beers will come from the likes of Batch Brewing and La Sirène, as well as breweries from across the Pacific, such as Deschutes.

58

— *The madcap beer* —
### FAFIK GRODZISKIE
Browar Artezan
Błonie, Poland
{ artezan.pl }
GRODZISKIE, 3-4%

Beer styles often go out of fashion. Ten years ago, the Polish smoked wheat beer Grodziskie seemed a goner. However, after prestigious Bamberg maltings Weyermann made oak-smoked malted wheat available again, several breweries prepared for a new adventure in brewing Grodziskie. Browar Artezan decided to be one of these, and Fafik was the result. Pale in color, this is brewed with 100% oak-smoked malted wheat which produces a subtle smokiness; allied with a high carbonation, this makes for a refreshing beer (New World hops give a delicate fruitiness).

— *The resurrectionist* —
### ORIGINAL LEIPZIGER GOSE
Gasthaus &
Gosebrauerei
Bayerischer Bahnhof
Leipzig, Germany
{ bayerischer-bahnhof.de }
GOSE, 4.5%

Gose is the sour wheat beer style that has been revived by many craft brewers, both in the United States and the UK, to become a symbol of their open-mindedness in making a beer that includes salt in the recipe. Yet it's at the railway station of Leipzig that Bayerischer Bahnhof's Gose roams, a hazy orangey-yellow beer with a delicately spicy and ozone-like nose. The palate is spicy, with the salt adding body to the mouthfeel, while the finish has boiled lemon sweetness with more salt and spice. It's refreshing and thirst-quenching.

— *Faith* —
### HOWLING PILS
Howling Hops
London, UK
{ howlinghops.co.uk }
PILSNER, 4.6%

For many British craft breweries, making a Czech-style Pilsner is as much an act of faith as it is an adventure. You need the correct raw materials, brewing technique and, most importantly, the necessary time to deliver a beer that will deceive drinkers into thinking that they are sitting in a cellar bar in Pilsen. Howling Hops, who make and serve their beer in the East End of London, have managed this sleight of hand with Howling Pils — their beer has a fullness, a spicy and sweet nose, gentle grainy toastiness on the palate, and a long dryness and bitterness in the finish.

*— Let's go to Düsseldorf —*
**NEU**
Orbit Beers
London, UK
{ orbitbeers.com }
DÜSSELDORF-STYLE
ALTBIER, 4.7%

Like a quiet soul gradually growing in confidence in putting forward his or her point of view, this South London take on the Altbiers of Düsseldorf becomes more assertive with every taste. Light chestnut-brown in color, it has a clean nose with hints of fruitiness and a slight spiciness, hence the shy start. However, on the palate, the beer starts to make sense, with an undercurrent of fruitiness reminiscent of cherry, a slight pepperiness, and a smooth and creamy mouthfeel before the lingering bitter finish makes its impression on the crowd gathered around.

*— Audacious and dashing —*
**VIÆMILIA**
Birrificio del Ducato
Busseto, Italy
{ birrificiodelducato.it }
PILSNER, 5%

Named after the ancient Roman road that ran between Rimini and Piacenza, this sprightly and frisky Pilsner has a similar sense of determined direction, but it's also an audacious and dashing beer, keen to swagger into your glass. Fresh and lemony on the nose, it has a caramel and lemon-like sweetness on the palate; it is soft and yielding in its mouthfeel, while a ramrod of dryness and bittersweetness stands up in the finish and conjures up images of small Czech villages where a beer like this can be drunk straight from the source. Each sip is a journey in itself.

*— Forget me not —*
**GADDS' NO. 3**
Ramsgate Brewery
Broadstairs, UK
{ ramsgatebrewery.co.uk }
BITTER, 5%

Sometimes it's easy to forget about the adventure that a solid English bitter, laced and fired by Kentish hops, can be. It's too easy to forget about that citrusy slow-build of sweetness, the worlds of toffee and hop spice on both nose and palate, the crosstown traffic of blistering bitterness and dryness, the siren call of English hops, the warp and weft of the raw materials, the full body. And as you delve deeper and deeper into a glass of Gadds' No. 3, you will realize so much how easy it is to forget the adventure that starts with a great bitter, and how much you miss it.

— *The pack-your-bags beer* —
## BARTHOLOMÄUS FESTMÄRZEN
Löwen Bräu Buttenheim
Buttenheim, Germany
{ loewenbraeu-buttenheim.de }
MÄRZEN, 5%

There's always a tingling sense of excitement
for beer travelers when they make it to a small
town where there's a brewery whose
reputation is larger than its structural
dimensions. That's the feeling the small
Franconian town of Buttenheim engenders,
since it is home to a tremendous brewpub
that produces a fine and elegant line of beers.
The Festmärzen is a worthy award for such an
adventure: golden in the glass, with a slight
and delicate nose of lemon citrus. It's a soft and
creamy lager with a touch of vanilla, and more
lemon before its soft and elegant bitterness.
This is a beer that, once drunk in its hometown,
makes it hard to leave the place.

— *Resolute* —
## KOUTSKA 12° SVĚTLÝ LEŽÁK
Pivovar Kout na Šumavě
Kout na Šumavě, Czech Republic
{ pivovarkout.cz }
PILSNER, 5%

Kout na Šumavě is a small town on the edge
of the Bohemian Forest, and it is believed that
the site of the eponymous brewery has been
home to brewing since the 17th century. The
communist regime closed the current brewery
in 1971, but a new owner in 2001 was resolute
in his plans for restoration, and beer began to
flow again. One of the beers is this gorgeous,
amber-gold, Czech-style pale lager, which has
herbal, mineral, and light caramel notes on the
nose, while each swig reveals a bready, herbal,
bittersweet, and dry beer that is hard to resist.

— *The dashing one* —
## PALE ALE
The Kernel Brewery
London, UK
{ thekernelbrewery.com }
PALE ALE, 5.2%
(ABV VARIES)

If it were ever possible to be privy to the thoughts of a brewer, we would be in for an interesting journey during the making of his or her pale ale. "In which direction shall we go? Which adventure do I want to experience with this pale ale?" would be the general tenor of the thoughts, for pale ale is not the simple beer style some might imagine it to be. It might be an English pale ale with its burnished copper hue, crisp outreach of malt, and muscular hop heft; or it could be American, where the bright colors of Yakima Valley hops leap out of the glass with the verve and velocity of a Fourth of July fireworks display. Kernel's pale ales have always had this sense of adventure, this sense of surprise and sunrise, especially as various expressions feature different hop varieties. (Kernel is not known for standing still, as its credo attests: "The brewery springs from the need to have more good beer.") It could be a blend, Centennial and Simcoe perhaps, bursting with tropical fruit lushness, or a hop all on its own, such as Hallertau Blanc, with its gush of gooseberry, grapes, and passion fruit on the nose. This all means that Kernel's pale ales are never the same, apart from one thing: they are juicy and fruity, bracing in their bitterness, easy to drink, and drenched in a lip-smacking succulence. Open a bottle, and the dash for adventure starts with a hiss.

— *One man's enterprise* —
### VIENNA
Cervejaria Bierland
Blumenau, Brazil
{ bierland.com.br }
VIENNA LAGER, 5.4%

Vienna: it means something to us. However, in the company of a glass of this crisp and gently toasty Vienna-style lager, with added citrus and floral notes from dry-hopping, we are drinking and celebrating the enterprise and ambition of pioneering brewer Anton Dreher. Born in Vienna, his travels to German and British breweries in the 1830s inspired him to develop an amber-colored beer that vied for bar-top supremacy with golden Pilsners throughout the 19th century. Bierland's version is a continuation of Dreher's vision.

— *The buccaneer* —
### PALE ALE
Pirate Life
Adelaide, Australia
{ piratelife.com.au }
PALE ALE, 5.4%

There's a swagger and a swerve in the way one of Adelaide's newest breweries makes its beer. Pale ale is unashamedly West Coast in inspiration, with a zap and a zest of bold American hops giving it tropical fruit high fives, a firm, bracing, and biscuity backbone finished with a life-affirming zing of bitterness and dryness that makes you want to swing from the rigging like a pirate about to set off on the adventure of a lifetime. And like all good pirates, this pale ale will soon be hitting the seven seas and landing on a shore near you.

— *Resolutely adventurous* —
### NOBLESSE
Brouwerij De Dochter
van de Korenaar
Baarle-Hertog, Belgium
{ www.dedochtervande
korenaar.be }
BELGIAN ALE, 5.5%

Baarle-Hertog is the hometown of this small family brewery on the border between the two main Low Countries, a curious enclave that is classed as Belgian but is actually in the Netherlands. Beer lovers wishing to experience such an international anomaly should make their way to the brewery where beers such as Noblesse can be enjoyed. Light golden in color, this beer is sure of its place in the world, with its delicate spice, light, honeyed sweetness balanced by a crisp dryness, and in the finish a long bitterness that awakens the palate.

*— The creative —*

## RETURN OF THE EMPIRE
Moor Beer
Bristol, UK
{ moorbeer.co.uk }
IPA, 5.7%

If we talk about IPAs, then the only thread making its way through the conversation will be about the intensity of the American hops used by brewers. Moor Beer's Justin Hawke is a creative brewer who loves the hops of his native United States, but with this bold big hitter of an IPA he has let a new English hop variety called Jester go on its own adventure. First brewed in 2012 as The Empire Strikes Back (hence its sequel of a name), the beer has a bowl full of ripe tropical fruit and squeezed citrus on the nose, alongside a crisp, biscuity sweetness; it's juicy and equally fruity on the palate, with a firm, lasting, bittersweet and dry finish.

*— The wanderer —*

## EVIL TWIN COWBOY
Evil Twin Brewing
Copenhagen, Denmark
{ eviltwin.dk }
PILSENER, 5.5%

Cowboys sitting around a campfire, the aroma of the smoke hanging in the air, a catch in the throat, a dryness that demands a beer. With this delicately smoked Pils, Danish gypsy brewery Evil Twin, founded by Jeppe Jarnit-Bjergsø, brother of craft brewer superstar Mikkel Borg Bjergsø, has aimed to evoke this mythical stage of a cowboy's life, the moments when the wandering briefly stops and there's time for reflection, and — naturally — a cold beer. Despite its celebration of smokiness, this is a very mellow beer that both refreshes and brings on dreams of the great outdoors.

"LET A MAN WALK TEN MILES STEADILY ON A HOT SUMMER'S DAY ALONG A DUSTY ENGLISH ROAD, AND HE WILL SOON DISCOVER WHY BEER WAS INVENTED."
G. K. CHESTERTON, 1915

— *The fearless adventurer* —
### HOP HOG
Feral Brewing
Perth, Australia
{ feralbrewing.com.au }
IPA, 5.8%

— *The adventure of ambition* —
### PORTER GOURMANDE
Les Brasseurs du Grand Paris
Paris, France
{ bgp.paris }
PORTER, 5.9%

Feral sounds like the mark of the fearless adventurer, the kind of person who likes to dive headfirst into a beer and savor its boldness and brashness. It is just as well that Hop Hog is that kind of beer — an American-style IPA brimming with tangy, tantalizing US hop character on both the nose and the palate.

Passion fruit, crisp, malty warmth and sweetness, grapefruit, buzzsaw bitterness, juicy fruitiness, and a dryness that wouldn't be out of place in some of the arid areas of Feral's home state of Western Australia. Feral are pretty fearless as well, which they probably have to be given that they make their beer in the heart of WA's wine-making territory, the Swan Valley.

How's this for ambition? In 2011 Anthony Baraff moved from the United States with his French wife to live in Paris. Previous visits had signaled a dearth of American-style hoppy beers, so he learned to home-brew. Once in Paris, he founded the self-styled nomad brewery Les Brasseurs du Grand Paris with the aim of converting Parisians to the joys of individual artisanal beers. As well as big hop bombs such as IPA Citra Galactique, he produced this silky-smooth porter, a dark seducer rich in coffee and chocolate flavors with a delicate undertow of vanilla coming alongside. Such has been the success of Baraff's ambitions that 2017 should see Les Brasseurs ensconced in its own brewery in Paris.

*— Discover the hop lager —*

### KESERŰ MEZ

Fóti Kézműves
Sörfőzde
Fót, Hungary
{ fotisorfozde.hu }
PILSENER, 6%

Hungary is best known for its cold blond lagers, but Keserú Mez is different from the norm — a strong lager with a gentle mouthfeel, a honeyed sweetness, and ferocious bitterness. Brewed by the compact Fóti Kézműves Sörfőzde in a village north of Budapest, this is one of the finest Hungarian artisanal beers and a sign of the brewery's ambitions — best demonstrated by its calling the beer a hop lager, an indigenous attempt at an American pale ale. It was brewed in 2011 and became an immediate hit with the small but growing band of Hungarian aficionados.

*— A century of adventure —*

### OUDE GEUEZE

Hanssens Artisanaal
Dworp, Belgium
{ lambic.info }
GUEUZE, 6%

Hanssens once produced lambic, and then lost their vessels to the invading German army in 1914, but when peace returned, the Hanssen family were determined to soldier on, this time as a blender of locally made lambics. This is how they have remained to this day, taking lambics from the likes of Boon and Giradin and then blending them and allowing the results to sleep the sleep of the just in ancient wooden barrels. The result is a beer of infinite complexity, tart, refreshing, funky, and full-bodied. Sometimes the adventure of beer is the time and the history it takes to make a world classic.

*— Adventurous education —*

### AUDIT ALE

Westerham
Crockham Hill, UK
{ westerhambrewery.co.uk }
STRONG ALE, 6.2%

Beer has had its own adventures in several UK colleges, especially when a strong ale was brewed to celebrate the annual audit of college accounts, hence the term "audit ale." Westerham's vinous version is based on one brewed during the 1930s by the Black Eagle Brewery (and supplied to Clarence House for the start of the oyster season). This is a well-assured beer with plenty of poise on the palate, and fruity, full-bodied, and satisfying in the finish.

*— It started with a brewery —*
## BOXING CAT TKO INDIA PALE ALE
Boxing Cat Brewery
Shanghai, China
{ boxingcatbrewery.com }
IPA, 6.3%

Shanghai-based Boxing Cat was founded in 2008 by three intrepid Americans, exiles who wanted a taste of the craft beers they loved so much at home. Their big adventure paid off, and Boxing Cat has grown to include three brewpubs in China's largest city where expats and locals can feast on TKO (or Technical Knock Out), one of its most highly regarded beers. TKO is a highly accomplished American-style IPA — juicy, citrusy, leafy, piny, bittersweet, and with a long, bitter finish. A beer for the adventurous, especially since it is not bottled, and rarely makes it out of China.

*— An adventure in D.C. —*
## PEPPERCORN SAISON
3 Stars
Washington, D.C., USA
{ 3starsbrewing.com }
SAISON, 6.5%

"What to put in a beer?" is a common refrain in the experimental hothouse of US craft brewing. Some brewers add honey, others fruit (and even veg), but over at 3 Stars it's peppercorns that are the adventurous ingredient in an equally adventurous beer style, saison. The result is a spicy, fruity, flinty beer with a creamy mouthfeel, a classic farmhouse beer that makes you think you are in the Wallonian countryside rather than the US federal capital. And those who make their way to D.C. will be well rewarded at the brewery tap — the Urban Farmhouse.

*— The rash lure of darkness —*
## MROK
Baba Jaga
Wrocław, Poland
{ Facebook: browarbabajaga }
BLACK IPA, 6.5%

What shall we drink today? How about a devil-may-care, robustly roistering Black IPA from a young brewery in the lively city of Wrocław in Poland? Baba Jaga only began making beers in 2015, and they depend on other breweries to produce them, but this does not lessen the swagger and dash with which their beers are invested. A thorough sense of freedom and adventure can be found in Mrok as roasted grain, pine, and citrus swirl out of the glass, while the palate is more pine and citrus and luscious dark malts, with a dry and bitter finish that asks the drinker to have another swig.

— *The dashing cavalier* —

**LA BLONDE
D'ESQUELBECQ**

Brasserie Thiriez

Esquelbecq, France

{ brasseriethiriez.com }

BIÈRE DE GARDE, 6.5%

This is a dashing, laughing cavalier of a beer (or should that be a roguish Republican, given that it is brewed in the northern heartlands of France?), scattering out aromatic bursts of juicy citrus on the nose, somewhat reminiscent of a Belgian Tripel. As if realizing the need to calm down, this bombshell of a blond settles on the palate with restrained citrus (plus hints of pineapple), a drying spiciness, an undercurrent of vanilla, a creamy mouthfeel, and a bittersweet finish with some crunchy biscuitiness adding muscle. It's elegant yet feisty, dashing, and dextrous.

— *The globe-trotter* —

**FRIDAY IPA**

And Union

Munich, Germany

{ andunion.com }

IPA, 6.5%

Where shall we go with Friday? To the United States or Germany? That's the conundrum posed by this American-style IPA that is brewed in Bavaria (the founders of brewers And Union are based in South Africa). Let's see if taste can help the choice of destination. It's dry and bitter with a biscuitiness often found in Bavarian bocks; there's a gentle toastiness and sweetish citrus on the nose, a Champagne-Moussec fullness on the palate, hints of orange marmalade, plus an intriguing juxtaposition between bitterness and sweetness before its dry and bracingly bitter finish.

— *Thoughtful swashbuckler* —

**DICHOTOMOUS DUBBEL**

Kettle Green Brewing

Melbourne, Australia

{ kettlegreenbrewing.com.au }

DUBBEL, 6.8%

Like a thoughtful swashbuckler who veers between action, introspection, and intoxication, this is a beer with three levels of understanding. It is brewed in Melbourne; being a Dubbel-style, it takes its inspiration from the Trappist monasteries of Belgium; finally, cold-brewed coffee made from the Ethiopian Yirgacheffe bean is added post-fermentation (the brewery has collaborated with a local coffee roaster). The result is a chivalrous, elegant beer in which the fruitiness of the Dubbel marries well with the smoothness and delicate spiciness of the coffee.

*— Audacious —*

### ČERNÁ RAKETA

Pivovar Matuška
Broumy, Czech
Republic
{ pivovarmatuska.cz }
BLACK IPA, 7%

*— Be bold, be brave —*

### GROSSE BERTHA

Brussels Beer Project
Brussels, Belgium
{ beerproject.be }
HEFEWEIZEN, 7%

*— Transatlantic —*

### CLOWN JUICE

Magic Rock Brewing
Huddersfield, UK
{ magicrockbrewing.com }
INDIA WIT ALE, 7%

The audacity of it all. Twenty-something Czech brewer Adam Matuška goes off and makes a Black IPA (uncommon in his country) that's bursting with flavor and promise, and renames it an India dark ale. Dark chestnut, beneath an ample head of foam, this incredibly drinkable beer has a rich fruity nose of citrus (orange, grapefruit) alongside a scattering of dark malts suggestive of coffee and chocolate. It's audaciously drinkable, especially considering its strength, with aromatic intensity replicated on the palate, and a dry and bitter finish.

When old friends Sébastien Morvan and Olivier de Brauwere began their project in 2013, they brewed their beers elsewhere using the crowd-funding model and Facebook to raise funds and gather support. It's obviously worked, and they now have their own brewery in the stylish Dansaert district of Brussels. Grosse Bertha is their self-styled Belgian Hefeweizen, with its classic Hefe note of cloves and banana fruit on the nose, joined by a spiciness (some pepper perhaps), herbal notes, and a tongue-livening effervescence on the palate. A classic hybrid that totally makes sense.

This is an adventure that bridges the Atlantic, combining the Witbier of Flanders with the hop-boosting IPA of the United States (and a defining dalliance with the West Coast), hence the brewery calling it an India Wit ale. Hazy orange in color, it has a bloom of orange juiciness and coriander spice on the nose, while a citrus juiciness, sandalwood sweetness, banana fruitiness, and peppery spice all work their way through the palate before the bitter and dry finish. It could easily be a mess, but in the hands of Magic Rock's master brewer, Stuart Ross, this adventure is worth signing up for.

— *Reckless* —

**FIRST FRONTIER**

To Øl

Copenhagen, Denmark

{ to-ol.dk }

IPA, 7.1%

First Frontier is a West Coast-style IPA, boisterous and bruising in its aromatics of peach and grapefruit, smooth and sluicing the palate with more tropical fruit, and refreshing and restorative in the way its finish is dry, bitter, fruity, and assertive. So far, so craft. Yet, what makes this a reckless, edge-of-the-seat beer is the way the founders set off on their adventure in a pale beer-obsessed Denmark, took the gypsy brewing route (this beer is brewed in Belgium at De Proefbrouwerij), and continue to brew beers they like. Drink this when you can, and experience the Danish beer revolution firsthand.

— *Swashbuckling* —

**WWA**

Browar Bazyliszek

Warsaw, Poland

{ browarbazyliszek.pl }

FOREIGN STOUT, 7.2%

Why WWA? "Whisky Wooden Ale" according to the brewery, in which a strong stout spends time within a wooden barrel that once held the water of life, and becomes fortified with its spirituality while also picking up notes of vanilla, peat, and smoke. The nomenclature of foreign stout is of a dark and bittersweet stout, stronger than average, smooth and creamy, sooty even, so when the former home-brewers Browar Bazyliszek, who are based just outside Warsaw, tried out this marriage we were gifted with a beer whose flavor is as deep as the Mariana Trench, and just as thrilling to immerse yourself in.

— *The river runs deep* —

**BUOY IPA**

Buoy Brewery

Astoria, OR, USA

{ buoybeer.com }

IPA, 7.5%

You can sit and drink glass after glass of this potent West Coast IPA at Buoy's brewery tap in Astoria where the wide-spanned Columbia River rushes to its ultimate destiny: the Pacific. However, even if you don't make your way to Astoria, you can imagine the sights and sounds of the river meeting the ocean when pouring yourself a bottle of this beer. Fresh tropical fruit, resiny pine, and an onion-like savoriness exist on the nose, while the palate has the tingle of tropical fruits such as mango and papaya, joined by a malt sweetness and grassiness before it tumbles into a brisk, dry, and cracker-like finish.

*— Intrepid —*
### HITACHINO NEST ESPRESSO STOUT
Kiuchi Brewery
Naka, Japan
{ hitachino.cc }
COFFEE STOUT, 7.5%

*— Fields of dreams —*
### TOURNAY NOIRE
Brasserie de Cazeau
Templeuve, Belgium
{ brasseriedecazeau.be }
STOUT, 7.6%

I was in a large, old 19th-century pub in Hackney, on the edge of Victoria Park, London, and I wanted something different from the IPA that I had been enjoying throughout a dull meeting, which had now finished. "How about this?" said the young barman, brandishing a bottle of Hitachino Nest Espresso Stout at me, "It's got coffee beans in it." It was a small stubby bottle, whose label was a mixture of swirling two-tone browns with a small bird in the middle. I nodded. The moment I drank the smooth, full-bodied, velvety, mocha-sweet, espresso-bitter, cracker-dry beer was like being an intrepid adventurer who had hacked his way through a jungle to arrive at a shining city of contentment. "Another?" said the barman a few minutes later. I nodded.

Brasserie de Cazeau, close to the city of Tournai in the province of Hainaut in Belgium, is a brewery of the land, based on an old farm, an island within a sea of fields, a place that you might just come upon as you roam the roads in search of who knows what. Sometimes adventure is about discovery, and discovering this big beer is one big adventure. As the name suggests, this is a dark beer sitting in the glass beneath a crema-colored head; it's potent on the palate—dark treacle and toffee, vanilla, a hint of burnt toast, some smoke, mocha coffee, milk chocolate, and a creamy mouthfeel, all followed by a grainy dryness in the finish. Grab a bottle and allow yourself to drift through the fields of Elysium.

## JAMBE-DE-BOIS

Brasserie de la Senne
Brussels, Belgium
{ brasseriedelasenne.be }
TRIPEL, 8%

Brasserie de la Senne moved into its home in
2009 and then took another year to complete
the work needed to start brewing. Until then,
founders Yvan De Baets and Bernard Leboucq
had made their beers at another brewery for
several years, an arrangement that landed them
with a proven track record for beers such as
Taras Boulba and Zinnebir. "We brew what we
want to drink," De Baets once told me. Creativity runs like a river through de la Senne's beers,
which have an appetizing bitterness that makes
them stand out from many other Belgian
brewers who use spices and candy sugar in
their recipes. Therefore, with this in mind, here
is the brewery's muscular Tripel, stripped of the
sweetness that all too often afflicts the more
commercial examples. It chimes and rings with
the angular pineapple-like fruitiness you get
from a Tripel, but there is an austereness that
you would expect from a monk. But let us not
forget that these monks can smile, as the hints
of banana-like esters suggest, all of which produce a weighty, austere, fat but not flabby and
bittersweet Tripel, demonstrative of De Baets's
and Leboucq's sense of creativity.

— *Brash and carefree* —

### FATAMORGANA
Omnipollo
Stockholm, Sweden
{ omnipollo.com }
IMPERIAL IPA, 8%

The Swedish duo of Henok
Fentie and Karl Grandin began
making beer in 2011 with the
help of like-minded
breweries around the world.
This is a conceptual project,
and it could so easily be an
emperor with no clothes,
but these are beers with
drive, quality, and
personality. Brewed at
Dugges Bryggeri in Sweden,
Fatamorgana is an Imperial
IPA with a big furnace blast
of tropical and citrus fruits
plus grass on the nose. A piny
resinous character joins the
fruitiness in the mouth, while
the addition of oats and wheat
adds a smoothness to the
texture. Go brash, go carefree,
go Omnipollo.

— *An imperious enterprise* —

### DOUBLE OATMEAL STOUT
Passarola Brewing
Lisbon, Portugal
{ passarola.pt }
IMPERIAL STOUT, 8%

Lisbon is a city that engenders
a sense of adventure and
exploration — roads run up
and down hills; automobiles
and trams share the same
space; small neighborhood
cafés are everywhere.
Passarola is based here, and
even though it doesn't have its
own brewery you could argue
that its beers mirror the
qualities of its home city.
Double Oatmeal Stout is an
Imperial, an imperious beer
even, with a minty, tarry,
creamy, vinous, coffee-like
character, a sense of its own
confidence. It shows that beer
adventures can be had in the
unlikeliest of cities.

— *Sandy adventures* —

### IMPERIAL PELICAN ALE
Pelican Pub & Brewery
Pacific City, OR, USA
{ pelicanbrewing.com }
IMPERIAL IPA, 8%

Down on Cannon Beach in
Pacific City, Oregon, where the
sand is golden and a quarter
of a mile out the Haystack
Rock emerges from the water
like a massive blunt stone
arrowhead, Pelican Pub &
Brewery stands. This is one
of the most idyllic places on
the US West Coast, where the
beer lover can open a bottle
of Imperial Pelican Ale and
contemplate the scenery. A
blare of citrus fruit and malt
sweetness emerges out of this
massive Imperial IPA. Sip after
sip reveals more citrus, pine, a
hop bitterness, the balance of
grain, and biscuity sweetness,
before it finishes with a
flourish of grand bitterness.

— *A swaggering star of an adventurer* —

## HEADY TOPPER

The Alchemist
Stowe, VT, USA
{ alchemistbeer.com }
IMPERIAL IPA, 8%

In the spirit of adventure I went beer-hunting in Vermont during the summer of 2010. One of my trips saw me looking for The Alchemist brewery in the village of Waterbury, where it had a brew-pub. Saturday lunchtime and a farmers' market were in full swing, but I had no luck in trying its beers as the brewpub was closed (owners and founder John and Jen Kimmich were still in Burlington at the Vermont Brewers' beer festival, where I had enjoyed their Imperial Pils the night before). Within a year, Waterbury was hit by Hurricane Irene and the pub and brewery were destroyed. However, just in time, the Kimmichs had also opened a brewing and canning facility from where Heady Topper emerged and proceeded to enchant and entrance beer lovers with its fresh and dynamic approach to the US style of Imperial IPA. For several years, this was the only beer produced by Alchemist, and the brewery was (and is) resolutely local in its distribution, with the aim being that drinkers enjoy Toppy Header only at its freshest. So basically you have to travel to enjoy it, or get a friend to bring it back to wherever you are in the world. Is it worth it? Of course it is, for it is a fresh, tropically fruity, exuberant, expletive-goading, hop-filled Imperial IPA that swaggers and sways in the glass as if it were Mick Jagger on the stage in his pomp. Tropical Storm Irene did the world of beer a great unexpected favor.

74

— *An aristocratic ale* —
## GULDENBERG
Brouwerij De Ranke
Dottignies, Belgium
{ deranke.be }
BELGIAN STRONG ALE,
8%

The name of this beer suggests an adventurous, but dissolute, 19th-century aristocrat who disgraced the family name and ended his life in penury. On the other hand, the beer in the glass tells a different tale, which is one of an herbal, spicy nose alongside a hint of licorice or even star anise. The carbonation is as frisky as a young foal let loose in a paddock for the first time; the mouthfeel is full-bodied, and there is dandelion and burdock, toffee, and a hint of sarsaparilla in the palate — a unity of flavor. The finish is dry, with a return of caramel.

— *Fearless* —
## OF FOAM AND FURY
Galway Bay Brewery
Galway, Ireland
{ galwaybaybrewery.com }
IMPERIAL IPA, 8.5%

This was supposedly the first Imperial IPA brewed in Ireland, and has become an iconic beer, irresistible in its charms in the glass. Inspired by American beers of the same ilk, it's an Errol Flynn–like swoop on the taste buds, from the big bold gusts of tropical fruit, pine resin, spikes of citrus, and malt-influenced sweetness on the nose to the equally complex matrix of fruit, pine, and malt on the palate. First drunk, it's a beer that stills conversation and inspires a consideration and veneration of the brewer's art, followed by a question: just how on earth does one get so much flavor and aroma into one beer?

— *Enterprising* —
## RUINATION 2.0
Stone Brewing
Escondido, CA, USA
{ stonebrewing.com }
IMPERIAL IPA, 8.5%

Ruination was first brewed in 2002, and it became a staple part of Stone Brewing's repertoire, an aggressively hopped Imperial IPA that helped give the brewery its global reputation. In 2015, the makers released what they called the beer's "second incarnation" — Ruination 2.0. The result is a fusillade of even more hop character, with tropical fruitiness, deep resiny pine, and bright and luminous citrus. Meanwhile, an ethereal malt-inclined sweetness provides the background for all these hop colors to be splashed upon. The brewery calls Ruination a "Liquid Poem to the Glory of the Hop."

## — *Risky* —
## PAPAYA CRASH
Nómada Brewing
Sabadell, Spain
{ nomadabrewing.com }
IMPERIAL IPA, 8.8%
(ABV VARIES)

The year 2011 saw Javier
Aldea and Sami Claret come
together and create Nómada,
and they were soon winning
plaudits for their beers, even
though they didn't have their
own brewery. Payapa Crash is
their bold and brash Imperial
IPA, a shimmering gold-
colored beer brimming with
the aromas of citrus, resin, and
white grapes with a graininess
in the background. It's equally
fruity when sipped, with a
bittersweet character, full
mouthfeel, and a luscious and
lubricious sense of its own
strength and character. The
brewery has made three
editions so far of the beer,
using different hops, all
of which have been well
received.

## — *Reckless* —
## GINORMOUS
Gigantic Brewing
Portland, OR, USA
{ giganticbrewing.com }
IMPERIAL IPA, 8.8%

This is a big, hoppy beer,
gigantic on the nose as well as
on the palate, delivering great
aromatic blasts of juicy orange
and resinous pine, before it's
time to dive into a deep pool
of flavor. There's plenty of
grapefruit and orange, and an
undercurrent of toffee
sweetness all wrapped up
with a savor and zip in the
long, dry, fruity finish. As for
Ginormous, the name refers
to the massive robot Ginormo
that appears on the bottle
label, fists clenched and eyes
flashing red, which is what
presumably happens if you're
reckless enough to drink too
much of this beast of a beer.

"THE GOOD LORD HAS CHANGED
WATER INTO WINE, SO HOW CAN
DRINKING BEER BE A SIN?"
SIGN NEAR A BELGIAN MONASTERY

76

*— Brassy —*

### PIKE MONK'S UNCLE TRIPEL

Pike Brewing
Seattle, WA, USA
{ pikebrewing.com }
TRIPEL, 9%

There's a kind of
contradiction about Pike
Monk's Uncle Tripel. It's a
Belgian-style Tripel, influenced
by the kind of beer that
Trappist monks make (the
yeast used comes from
Westmalle). It is full-bodied,
bittersweet, and rich, and
chimes with peachy-apricot
honeyed notes on both nose
and palate. However, it is also
brewed in the midst of the
boisterous and brassy Pike
Place Market in Seattle. This is
a place for tourists and locals,
many of whom end up at the
brewery's tap room where this
beer is the perfect restorative
after the adventure that is
shopping in Pike Place.

*— The Brazilian Way —*

### PERIGOSA IMPERIAL IPA

Bodebrown
Curitiba, Brazil
{ bodebrown.com.br }
IMPERIAL IPA, 9.2%

Bodebrown was founded in
2009 in Curitiba, a city in the
southern state of Paraná, an
area in which many German
migrants had settled in the
past, influencing the local beer
traditions. Bodebrown, however, have done things their
way, with a series of
US-influenced beers such as
this Imperial IPA, one of the
first to be brewed in Brazil.
Gusts of tropical fruit emerge
out of the glass, while there's
mango, grapefruit, and juicy
orange on the palate, alongside
a firm malt background, before
it glides to a big, bitter, and
hoppy finish that lingers with
the force of a beautiful dream.

*— Potent and plucky —*

### BARLEY WINE

Antares
Mar del Plata,
Argentina
{ cervezaantares.com }
BARLEY WINE, 10%

Better known for its wines
and ice-cool lagers,
Argentina was introduced to
beers of depth, ambition, and
perception when Antares set
up a brewpub in the seaside
resort of Mar del Plata in 1998.
More outlets have followed
throughout the country. This
barley wine is dark amber in
color, with nutty, fruity-sweet
aromatics on the nose, while
it is full-bodied and creamy in
the mouth with further fruit,
some spice, alcohol heat, and
caramel-like sweetness before
its hop-ridden, proudly bitter
finish. A beer with which to
savor and toast the
continuing success of Antares.

— *The ardent adventurer* —
## PORTER BALTIQUE
Microbrasserie Les
Trois Mousquetaires
Brossard, Canada
{ lestroismousquetaires.ca }
BALTIC PORTER, 10%

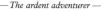

Porter Baltique was first
brewed in 2008 as a contrast
to the many Imperial stouts
that breweries in Quebec were
then making. It was originally
meant to be a seasonal, but
its popularity made it
available all the time. This is
a beer as dark as a moonless
night, potent and powerful
with dark rich notes of coffee,
chocolate, toffee, demerara
sugar, roasted grain, and a
smooth smokiness on both
the nose and the palate, the
latter thanks to the use of
a certain amount of
cherrywood-smoked malt.
There is also an oak-aged
version of the beer, released
annually in September.

— *Ra Ra Rasputin* —
## RASPUTIN
Brouwerij de Molen
Bodegraven,
Netherlands
{ brouwerijdemolen.nl }
IMPERIAL STOUT, 10.4%

This was de Molen's first
attempt at an Imperial stout.
The result is passionate and
soothing in the glass, with
plenty of chocolate, coffee,
dark fruits, caramel, roastiness, licorice, and bittersweetness. It's an expressive
beer, dark-as-midnight, thick
and full-bodied. When this
Herculean beer was launched
in the United States, a
Californian brewery objected
to the name because it made
a beer called Old Rasputin.
The brewery, tongue firmly
in cheek perhaps, renamed it
Disputin. The same sense of
fun can be seen on the label,
where it recommends that it
be enjoyed within 25 years.

— *Let's go!* —
## KAIJU! WHERE STRIDES
## THE BEHEMOTH
Kaiju Beer
Dandenong, Australia
{ kaijubeer.com.au }
BLACK IPA, 10.5%

There's a moment in the 2013
cult movie *Pacific Rim* when
one of the massive
kaiju-fighting Jaeger robots
smacks a fist into the palm of
its other hand, in anticipation
of the battle to come. This
robust and potent Black IPA
has a similar effect, as
aromatics of roast grain,
mocha coffee, chocolate, and
orange peel rise upward; the
taste is similarly monstrous,
an adventure of mocha,
chocolate, licorice, citrus,
and hints of rum alongside
a dense, viscous mouthfeel
before it finishes dry and
bitter, the smack of a massive
fist against an invading kaiju.

WHOEVER THOUGHT A BEER COULD
BE METAPHYSICAL OR COULD HAVE
SOMETHING TO SAY BEYOND ITS APPEAL
TO THE SENSES? THESE BEERS DO: THEY
ARE TUNEFUL, MUSICAL, DELICATE,
THOUGHTFUL, AND CONSIDERED,
ROMANTIC EVEN.

**POETIC**

## BARCELONA BEER FESTIVAL
Barcelona, Spain
March
{ barcelonabeerfestival.com }

Good beer is growing in importance in Barcelona, as this springtime festival, which began in 2011, demonstrates. It is held in a vast space, which is part of the old boatyards where Philip of Spain built the Armada. Here more than 300 beers from Spanish artisanal breweries can be sampled, alongside a judicious selection from new-wave brewers around the world. There is great food, a friendly and lively atmosphere, and a program of talks and meet-the-brewer events as well.

## BRISBANE BEER FEST
Brisbane, Australia
April
{ facebook.com/brisbanebeerfest.com.au }

More than 130 beers and ciders are available during this annual beer event, which is held over a weekend in April at Albion Park racetrack. It's a rambunctious festival that features some of the most highly regarded craft beers in Queensland, along with others from outside the state. As well as the awesome ales, there's music and great food — it's a fun atmosphere, and as soon as it finishes those who attended start to look forward to the next one.

## ZYTHOS BEER FESTIVAL
Leuven, Belgium
April
{ zbf.be }

Zythos is one of the biggest Belgian beer festivals, with more than 100 Belgian brewers bringing 500 different beers to an event center just outside Leuven. The beers, which come from independent breweries all over the country, are big and bold and (perhaps because many of them have sufficient alcoholic strength to make an ox tipsy) are served in measures of 10 ml (2 tsp). This makes it all the easier to taste and contemplate more beers than if they were being served in larger glasses.

## VERMONT BREWERS FESTIVAL
Burlington, VT, USA
July
{ vtbrewfest.com }

This annual two-day event is held within the well funky city limits of Burlington, and even better, it is out in the open, on Waterfront Park next to Lake Champlain, with drinkers afforded a glimpse of the mountains of New York state as the evening light crumbles. Naturally, it's a celebration of the beers of Vermont (as well as guests from Quebec, such as Dieu du Ciel), so expect beers from the likes of Rock Art, Hill Farmstead, Von Trapp, and Lawson's Finest Liquids.

## SYDNEY CRAFT BEER WEEK
Sydney, Australia
October
{ sydneycraftbeerweek.com }

This is not just one beer festival, but a series of events held across Sydney over nine days in October. There are tastings, tap takeovers by various breweries, celebrations, beer and food dinners, and beer educational events. The inaugural Sydney Craft Beer Awards, where stand-out achievements in beer are awarded, took place in 2016. It's lively and fun, both celebratory and cerebral, and as good a reason as any to visit the city during this period.

## CELTIC BEER FESTIVAL
St. Austell, UK
November
{ staustellbrewery.co.uk }

On a Saturday in late November, Cornish family brewery St. Austell organizes its annual Celtic Beer Festival, which is held in cellars beneath the main brewery. First held in 1999, it's a jamboree of more than 180 beers from St. Austell (including their experimental small batch range), the southwest, England, Wales, and Scotland, as well as a sizeable amount of ciders. It's a magnificent event that attracts fans from all over, and when the music starts in the afternoon, people never stop dancing.

*— Goethe's tipple? —*
### PINTA KWAS BETA
Browar PINTA
Wrocław, Poland
{ browarpinta.pl }
LICHTENHAINER, 3.2%

This beer is brewed in Wrocław, Poland, but in a style that originally came from Lichtenhain, over the border in Germany. Until recently, the Lichtenhainer was a dead style, remembered by a few, memorialized in the odd brewing text (perhaps Goethe drank it when he lived in Jena). It is a smoked beer, one of the sour beers of central-eastern Europe (similar to Gose, Grodziskie, or Berliner Weiss). Pinta's version is gold in color, slightly hazy, a fading sunset; the smokiness is delicate, like the remains of a wood fire in the morning. It's tart, gently puckering on the palate, playful, with some lemon, and a thirst-quenching dry finish.

*— The lightness of being —*
### LEMON ALE
Nørrebro Bryghus
Copenhagen, Denmark
{ noerrebrobryghus.dk }
SPECIALITY BEER, 3.5%

As the name might suggest, this is not a belt-and-braces beer or a tongue stripper in which hops stomp up and down the palate in the manner of a platoon of Grenadier Guards. Instead there's an ethereal lightness about it, a delicacy that is suggestive of a feather drifting on a breeze. It's a thirst-quencher, a friendly hand on the shoulder, a beer for the day, a beer that has had lemongrass, lime leaves, and ginger added to it, letting loose a fresh waft of lemon on the nose, while the palate is citrus, spice, and sweetness all coming together and suggesting that this is an ideal beer for reposing in a city park on a hot summer's day and musing on life.

*— Intrigue + complexity + time —*

## SOURDOUGH
Wild Beer
Westcombe, UK
{ wildbeerco.com }
SOUR BEER, 3.6%

Let's quote Wild Beer's co-founder Andrew
Cooper on the brewing philosophy that has
made this Somerset brewery one of the most
exciting outfits in recent years: the production
of sour beers is about "trying to add layers of
intrigue and complexity with time spent barrel
aging; the beers are ready when they are ready."
There's a sense of poetry and musicality in this
approach, creativity and ambition. Take
Sourdough for instance, which is loosely
based on Berliner Weiss. This is brewed with
a 58-year-old sourdough culture and it goes
straight into oak fermenters, bypassing the
usual destination of stainless steel; and then
it receives five months of maturation. It's pale
gold in color, and has a brisk carbonation that
is somewhat reminiscent of champagne; there's
a light acetic sourness on the nose alongside
hints of apple and citrus. The mouthfeel is
filling, a reminder of champagne, while there is
lemon, a gently beguiling sourness, and a tart
and thirst-quenching finish that invites you to
keep drinking.

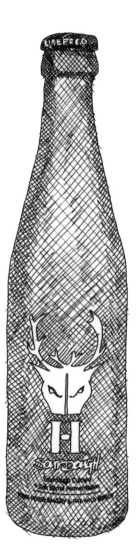

SEVEN MOODS OF CRAFT BEER · POETIC

— *London pride* —
### LONDON SOUR
The Kernel Brewery
London, UK
{ thekernelbrewery.com }
BERLINER WEISSE,
3.8%

I once sat down with Kernel's founder, Evin O'Riordan, and talked about London and beer while sipping a sour named after the capital city. I was immediately in tune with this beer: based on a Berliner Weisse, it's tangy, tart, juicy, and gently sour, with an aroma reminiscent of fruit-chew sweetness, followed by a dry and thirst-quenching finish. "We brew beers that we enjoy drinking," O'Riordan said to me, and at that moment it seemed that there was harmony in the world (for further rhapsody, London Sour has expressions featuring various fruits).

— *Romantic poetry* —
### BACIAMI LIPSIA
Birrificio del Ducato
Busseto, Italy
{ birrificiodelducato.it }
GOSE, 4%

Romance lives on with this beer, whose name translates as "Kiss me, Lipsia." You might think this odd, but its name seems appropriate even if it is a sour beer (a Gose to be more accurate). But what's love got to do with it? This is a sour beer with a light body (and a light gold color), an appetizing tartness, a fruitiness reminiscent of the sourness of biting into something like a physalis (initial tartness followed by elegant sweetness), which perhaps mirrors the sweet and sour nature of love, the yearning, the longing, the ups and downs of love's complexities.

— *A rhyme in beer* —
### SALTY KISS
### GOOSEBERRY GOSE
Magic Rock Brewing
Huddersfield, UK
{ magicrockbrewing.com }
GOSE, 4.1%

My initial introduction to Salty Kiss was far from sublime. I was in a London pub, and the beer was served through an infuser filled with gooseberries (to increase the gooseberry hit in a beer that already contained the fruit alongside sea buckthorn and salt). Thankfully, next time I drank it (this time from a can) the beer chimed and rhymed its way along my palate, with its counterpoint of ripe gooseberry and a briny day by the sea on the nose and a gently sour, zesty fruitiness, a hint of salt, and a dry tart finish when tasted.

— *A paean to Citra* —
## BUXTON SPA
Buxton Brewery
Buxton, UK
{ buxtonbrewery.co.uk }
GOLDEN ALE, 4.1%
❧

There's a simplicity about
Buxton's exemplary golden
ale SPA, especially when you
consider that the brewery is
also known for walking on the
wild side when it comes to
brewing. This beer, though, is
a love song: a lyrical paean, a
celebration of the Citra hop.
This is a beer bubbling with
juicy, citrusy (grapefruit and
lemon) notes on the nose,
while this luscious fruitiness
is also apparent in the taste,
alongside a bittersweet
graininess, and a dry and
bitter finish. It rings, it chimes,
it chatters away in the glass.

— *Rhapsody in wit* —
## GENTLEMAN'S WIT
Camden Town
London, UK
{ camdentownbrewery.com }
BELGIAN-STYLE
WITBIER, 4.3%
❧

I first tried this rhapsodic beer
back in 2011 when it was new
and I was visiting the brewery
for the first time (after being
bought by A-B InBev in 2015,
it has grown and grown). Here
was a Witbier served straight
from the tank. However, it
was not just a Witbier, but one
that had been infused with
lemons baked with bergamot
oil. Waves of coriander, lemon,
and a light pepperiness rolled
and rhymed across my mouth,
accompanied, chaperoned
even, by a soft, gentle
carbonation and a dry and
thirst-quenching finish. The
beer's harmony is a delight.

"GOD HAS A BROWN VOICE, AS
SOFT AND FULL AS BEER."
ANNE SEXTON, 1962

*— Galaxies will tremble —*
## TRADEWIND LAGER
Akasha Brewing Company
Five Dock, NSW, Australia
{ akashabrewing.com.au }
PILSENER, 4.4%
❧

*— Doggerel —*
## BAM NOIRE
Jolly Pumpkin Artisan Ales
Dexter, MI, USA
{ jollypumpkin.com }
SAISON, 4.5%
❧

The name of this beer comes from the zephyrs that created the trade routes that opened up the world to sea exploration. The beer itself is a reflection of this sense of movement: it's a pale lemony gold that shimmers in the glass beneath its fresh-fall-of-snow white head. Galaxy hops have been added, a southern hemisphere strain bursting with passion fruit and citrus, which, when combined with a mid-palate sweetness and a dry finish, declare this beer a well-cherished thirst-quencher. Drink this, gulp this, swig it, for it's as desirable as the coming of a fair wind that would take you to the Sydney suburb where this beer is made.

Bam is a cheeky-looking Jack Russell terrier who has inspired several of Jolly Pumpkin's beer names, including this one. It is a dark Saison, an ale of a farmhouse where the lights have just been extinguished, but look! There's a flicker of candlelight in the window, a glint, a tint of light amid the darkness. Imagine the same thing with this beer, dark until you hold it up to the light, and spy the reddish tints at the edge of the glass. There's a soft puckering of the palate, a gentle sourness, while there is also earthiness, peppery spice, light roast notes, a wisp of sweetness, ripe plum, and a tart, thirst-quenching finish.

— *Barcelona's architectural poetry* —
### FLOR DE LA VIDA
Edge Brewing
Barcelona, Catalonia, Spain
{ edgebrewing.com }
PALE ALE, 4.7%

Pale ale. The word "pale" suggests a ghost, or the face of Ophelia as she floats downstream, never to love again. And yet, when it comes to beer, a pale ale is golden-colored, veering toward copper at times, but never ghostly, as a glass of this crisp and lean but muscular pale ale demonstrates. There's a malt-derived sweetness at the start, a ping of sweetness, before a swoop of citrus and herbal notes (an eagle of hoppiness) that then leads on to a brisk, dry finish. It's an easy beer, a friendly beer, a rhyme of hops and malt that contrasts well with the architectural poetry of its home city.

—*Wandering lonely as a cloud* —
### PÄFFGEN KÖLSCH
Hausbrauerei Päffgen
Cologne, Germany
{ paeffgen-koelsch.de }
KÖLSCH, 4.8%

If Wordsworth were still alive and writing verse, he would have enjoyed the cloud-like lightness of the Kölsch beer style (sadly he died in 1850, 33 years before Hausbrauerei Päffgen started making beer). This is a beer that wanders across the palate, like a cloud across the sky, perceptible but light in its impact on the imagination. Maybe this is the appeal of Kölsch, of which Päffgen's is one of the most characteristic examples. Light golden in color, it has brisk carbonation, subtle citrus fruit, mid-palate sweetness, a refreshing character, and a light bitter finish. Sometimes we need our beers to be light and subtle — this is a great example.

SEVEN MOODS OF CRAFT BEER    POETIC

*— Light words, whispered gently —*
### YUZILLA PHANTOM
Beavertown Brewery
London, UK
{ beavertownbrewery.co.uk }
GOSE, 4.8%

Yuzilla Phantom is part of Beavertown's series influenced by Gose and Berliner Weiss, all of which started off with Lemon Phanton ("That was based on a love of the wonderful hangover cure Lemon Fanta!" the brewery's founder Logan Plant once told me). Yuzilla is a riff on Leipziger Gose, with dried limes, sea salt, and yuzu juice added, all of which create a tart, lightly fruity, just-over-the-horizon-saltiness thirst-quencher that is a phantom in the glass. It's light and delicate, zen-like in its zest, pale yellow in the glass, and refreshing in its wisp of sourness.

*— Rare beasts, and where to find them —*
### KUEHNES BLONDE
Kuehn Kunz Rosen
Mainz, Germany
{ kuehnkunzrosen.de }
WITBIER, 4.9%

This is a rare German beast: a Belgian-style Witbier. It's a silky, spicy, juicy beer with added coriander, orange peel, and grains of paradise as well as oats. It dances on the tongue, strikes poses, lifts the spirit, sifts all secrets. There's a gracefulness about its poise, an elegance about its refreshment, a softness about the way it lays its carbonation on the tongue, as if it was an eloquent love poem, or maybe a study of a flower, written sparingly at first but then followed by a rich rush of words as it finishes crisp and dry.

— *Edgar Allan Poe presents* —
## NAPAR PILS
Naparbier
Noáin, Spain
{ naparbier.com }
PILSNER, 4.9%

The label on Napar Pils brings to mind the poetry of Edgar Allan Poe. For a start, there's a skeleton with a beret on his head, and a scarf and an ax on his shoulder. The label is stylized, daubed in comic-book dark colors, and the skeleton has a toothpick between its teeth. The beer pours a pale, slightly hazy gold; the nose is a mellowed lemoniness, slightly oily in its effect, almost like the aroma of freshly cut grass. On the palate, it's fresh and refreshing, tangy and bitter. It is a beer with a great character, boosted by its dry and grainy finish. And then, like one of Poe's characters in search of what is troubling them, the dirty lemony note in the mid-palate is intriguing, rapturous, and rugged. Evermore.

"FOR A QUART OF
ALE IS A DISH FOR A
KING."
WILLIAM SHAKESPEARE,
*A WINTER'S TALE*, 1623

*— A haiku of dark malts —*
## TOKYO BLACK PORTER
Yo-Ho Brewing Company
Nagano, Japan
{ yohobrewing.com/e }
PORTER, 5%

This porter is like a haiku in a glass. Stygian in color, its darkness brings to mind the ferryman Charon, whom the dead pay to ferry them across the Styx to Hades, while chestnut-brown glints at the edge of the glass suggest redemption and restitution. There's a sweet siren call of caramel, vanilla, mocha, chocolate, and a hint of licorice on the nose, a hymnal of flavors that is continued on the palate. The sweetish, slightly roasty finish tingles with faint coffee notes. This is a beer, first brewed in 2005, which was developed by former head brewer Toshi Ishii, who learned his craft at Stone Brewing, a brewery equally adept at producing poems in a glass.

*— Boldly flavored beer needs bold words —*
## HOPFENSTOPFER CITRA ALE
Häffner Brau
Bad Rappenau, Germany
{ brauerei-haeffner.de }
PALE ALE, 5.1%

Most people assume that German brewers make only lager and Weissbier, but to quote a Nobel laureate: "the times they are a-changin'." Increasingly, German beer makers are being influenced by American craft brewing and Häffner Brau's master brewer Thomas Wachno is one of them. As well as making Pils, Export, and Weizen, he produces boldly hopped beers under the Hopfenstopfer (dry-hopped) label, one of which is Citra Ale. It's hazy orange-gold, and the nose has a delicate waft of ripe white grape and sweet banana. The mouthfeel has a Moussec-like creaminess, while the palate's white grape and Parma violet notes are kept in line by the bracingly bitter spine before the dry and fruity finish.

*— Let us go down to the sea —*
### KIWANDA CREAM ALE
Pelican Pub & Brewery
Pacific City, OR, USA
{ pelicanbrewery.com }
CREAM ALE, 5.2%

Sometimes when drinking beer it pays to imagine you are somewhere else — in the case of this refreshing, gold-colored beer, take yourself to the Pacific Ocean. Located in Oregon, the Pelican Pub and Brewery are right down on the beach facing the warm swell of the Pacific, and as you gulp (never sip: this is a drinking beer) this modern interpretation of a 19th-century beer style continues to play with your fancies. As you enjoy the light and delicate fruitiness, Moussec-like mouthfeel and bittersweet finish of this cream ale, you should feel the cool winds of the Pacific Ocean on your skin.

*— A favorite, well-read poem —*
### WEIHENSTEPHANER HEFE WEISSBIER
Bayerische Staatsbrauerei
Weihenstephan
Freising, Germany
{ weihenstephaner.de }
WEISSBIER, 5.4%

This is one of the oldest beers in the book, having first been brewed in 1933, but there's a sinuousness and lyricism about it that deserve to be celebrated once more. The nose is a tribute to classic Weissbier aromatics of bubblegum, banana, and cloves, with hints of lemon in the background; it pours a lemony gold with a thick solid band of cotton-wool white foam; bananas, clove, additional bubblegum, and a hint of spice produce a tingly sprightly palate; the finish offers further spice, bubblegum, biscuity maltiness, and a palpable sense of refreshment.

— *Drink while writing a limerick* —
### HAPPY OTTER
Cerveza Dougall's
Liérganes, Cantabria, Spain
{ dougalls.es }
PALE ALE, 5.6%

— *The Devil's trill* —
### CHROME SATAN
Hilliard's Brewing Company
Seattle, WA, USA
{ hilliardsbeer.com }
PRE-PROHIBITION LAGER, 5.7%

Happy Otter sounds like a character from a childhood rhyme or limerick. In fact, it celebrates Maris Otter, the malt variety that had its 50th birthday in 2015. Known as the Grand Cru of barley, Maris Otter gives a rich and rounded malt character whenever it is used. This is evident in this pale ale which was brewed to celebrate the same anniversary. However, it became so popular that it was changed from a one-off to a regular beer. The Maris Otter provides a solid backbone of caramel and sweetness upon which intimations of tingling peach, grapefruit, and juicy orange travel, livening the palate and leading toward a refreshing bittersweet finish.

I remember visiting Hilliard's. Cans were being filled, four at a time: caramel-colored beer with a flecked head of foam, before a movement of the machine forward saw the foam flicked off, smoothed, and a top added. It was sunny outside, and light flooded the brewery, a former garage, through big windows. Then I was handed a can of Chrome Satan, a pre-Prohibition lager. Amber in color, it had hints of caramel, a grainy dryness, a brush of sweetness mid-palate, and was light and easy to drink — a perfect match for the sun streaming in. (In the summer of 2016, Hilliard's was bought by fellow Seattle brewery Odin, and Chrome Satan is now brewed at their facility.)

— *Pop lyricism* —
### POP
Le Baladin
Piozzo, Italy
{ baladin.it }
PALE ALE, 5.7%

POP is the right word for this bright and cheery beer, which comes in multi-colored cans — a nod to pop art, perhaps. It was a change of direction for a brewery noted for its innovative use of yeasts, spices, and cereals. POP turns to the hop for a simple but surging American pale ale, which also celebrates the dry hopping dynamism of Mosaic and Cascade, both produced in Italy. The result is a spicy, citrusy beer, with plenty of peaks and troughs on the palate, an up and down of flavor before the final flatliner of bitterness, dryness, and fruitiness.

— *Light music* —
### MANGO HEFEWEIZEN
Durham Brewery
Durham, UK
{ durhambrewery.co.uk }
WEISSBIER, 5.8%

Adding mango to a riff on the classic Bavarian Hefeweizen takes us into fruit cocktail territory, as the beer style already has banana notes on the nose due to the yeast strain used. Durham Brewery, however, is very happy in its fruitful quest to produce a beer that mashes up Bavaria with Carmen Miranda's hat. The result is a refreshing and tropically tantilizing take on a Bavarian classic that would wake up the sleepiest of palates. Alongside the hints of banana and cloves, the subtlety of the mango adds an extra-fruity and refreshing dimension to this celebratory and tuneful beer.

— *A paean to bitterness* —
### DE RANKE XXX BITTER
Brouwerij De Ranke
Dottignies, Belgium
{ deranke.be }
BELGIAN ALE, 6%

There is a multitude of meanings to the word "bitterness," most of which are negative. But here bitterness is a pleasure, a positive embrace as a result of the hops used. De Ranke's XXX Bitter was a huge sensation in the Belgium beer market when it first appeared in the late 1990s. It was a bitter beer, standing out against a tide of sweetness. It remains a star, with aromatics of resin, pineapple, and fruit gums on the nose, and a well-rounded mouthfeel featuring additional tropical fruity and resin notes as well as a hint of woodiness before it finishes complex in its bitterness.

*— The annual serenade —*
### ENSORCELLED
The Rare Barrel
Berkley, CA, USA
{ therarebarrel.com }
SOUR BEER, 6.2%

Once a year, like the welcome return of a familiar migrating bird, Rare Barrel's Ensorcelled appears, eagerly anticipated by those in love with all things sour. A dark-colored blend that has been aged with raspberries, this is a perfect marriage of jammy raspberry notes, light chocolate, and toastiness, alongside a crisp tartness and a thirst-quenching and refreshing finish. It's a beer that fully deserves its name, which also means enchantment, a process that you could argue stretches out to the whole modus operandi of Rare Barrel, all of whose beers are sour blends of varying complexities.

*— Poetry of malt and hops —*
### BIBOCK
Birrificio Italiano
Lurago Marinone, Italy
{ www.birrificio.it }
HELLER BOCK, 6.2%

Amber orange in color, this beer is a fragrant, creamy, fruity, big-hearted, bittersweet variation on the Heller Bock style. When Birrificio Italiano started in 1996, the Italian beer scene was very different from today. Beers like this are a tribute to the foresight of founder Agostino Arioli, who told me: "When I started it was quite difficult, there were no suppliers for raw materials. My father knew someone in the brewing industry and I was given certain supplies — at the time I was using bakers' yeast, which wasn't that good." Now, Arioli is recognized as a master of his craft, whose beers sing with the poetry of malt and hops.

*— "God has a brown voice" —*
### ANGRY BOY BROWN ALE
Baird Brewing
Numazu, Japan
{ bairdbeer.com }
AMERICAN-STYLE
BROWN ALE, 6.2%

There are very few poems about the color brown (although Anne Sexton believed that "God has a brown voice, as soft and full as beer"), but the color does have its poetic side — the gleam of a well-polished sideboard, the rich rust-russet brownness of fallen leaves. And then there is this US-style brown ale: light chestnut in color, it has a wisp of caramel, brown sugar, vanilla, and hints of citrus on the nose, while, once swigged, it distracts the palate with a spicy, herbal, bittersweet presence before it finishes long, fruity, and with a restrained spiceness. How brown, how beautiful.

— *Magical Prague* —
### SVATÝ NORBERT IPA
Klášterní Pivovar Strahov
Prague, Czech Republic
{ klasterni-pivovar.cz }
**IPA, 6.3%**

It's a steep walk up from the Castle District
to this brewpub and restaurant, which has a
monastery as a neighbor. Imagine walking up
to it on a misty winter's night, when magical
Prague seems to tiptoe over the cobbles, and,
once in the main bar amid the gleaming copper
brewing kit, ordering a glass of this resiny,
citrusy, and bitter Czech IPA, in which the grapefruit cuts through the palate, and there are
thick chunks of peel, a refrain of refreshment,
while the bitterness in the finish is broad and
majestic. And while you drink, think about the
city and its people stretched out before you: the
history, the voices, and the way beer has a hold
on Prague.

— *The saintly savor of barley* —
### SEEFBIER
Antwerpse Brouw Compagnie
Antwerp, Belgium
{ seef.be }
**BELGIAN ALE, 6.5%**

This is an Antwerp beer, its owners proclaim,
although it is brewed elsewhere in Flanders
(there are crowd-funding plans for an Antwerp
site). I drank it in an Antwerp bar called The
11th Commandment, where shelves and
shelves of plaster saints of all shapes and sizes
look down on drinkers, commanding them
perhaps to savor the juice of the barley.
And amid this heavenly scene I discovered
a delightfully fruity and refreshing beer with
an effervescent mouthfeel, delicate banana
notes on the nose, and pineapple chunks on
the palate before a
pleasing bitter finish.

*— A hymn of praise —*

### CLOUDWATER WINTER RANGE — AUS HOPFEN WEISSE

Cloudwater Brew Co.
Manchester, UK
{ cloudwaterbrew.co }
HOPFENWEISSE, 6.5%

Manchester brewery Cloudwater changes its beer range with the seasons, which means that there have been several variations on the Hopfenweisse style, including one made with Mosaic, another with bergamot lemons, and this one with Australian hops, which came out in winter. This eclectic approach is a sign of adventure and exploration, an indication of how seriously they take their beers. This version of their Hopfen Weisse is hazy orange-gold in color, with passion fruit, ripe peach skin, lemon, and a hint of savoriness (perhaps asafoetida) on the nose, although the juicy fruitiness is the dominant characteristic. There is also some banana and an earthy hoppiness. Tropical fruit, including passion fruit, as well as a peppery spiciness, appear on the palate, alongside a juicy fruitiness and a bitterness that make it feel more grown-up than it should be. There is good carbonation, and a full-bodied mouthfeel before it finishes dry and woody, with tropical fruit and white pepper hanging around. This is a fascinating beer, complex and rewarding, a hymn to the excellence of British brewing.

*— The knell of parting day —*
## BROKEN DREAM
Siren Craft Brew
Finchampstead, UK
{ sirencraftbrew.com }
STOUT, 6.5%

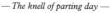

Siren dubs this lusciously creamy and smooth beer a breakfast stout (presumably because it contains coffee), but I would suggest that it is later in the day when its truly tranquil and creative nature is revealed (a mid-afternoon libation, perhaps; a refreshing stimulant to lift what remains of the day). This is a lyrical beer with ground coffee, treacle, chocolate, caramel, wafts of smoke from a coffee roaster, and soft brushes of vanilla on the nose, while every sip reveals additional coffee, vanilla, chocolate, and smoke alongside an espresso-like bitterness and a dryness in the finish.

*— Theme —*
## FLEMISH KISS
The Commons Brewery
Portland, OR, USA
{ commonsbrewery.com }
SOUR BEER, 6.5%

As I walked through the Belmont district of Portland on a hot summer's day I came upon Commons in a big old redbrick former warehouse. Inside stood a stripped-wood bar that featured Commons' devotion to French, Belgian, and German beer styles. Flemish Kiss was on draft and a pale ale combined with Brettanomyces appealed. Pale gold in color, with a fluffy head of foam, there was a gentle earthiness on the nose, alongside delicate lemon notes; more citrus and tropical fruit and sourness on the palate, combined with a brisk Moussec-like mouthfeel before the dry finish.

*— A glass of serenity —*
## FALKON KAMŠOT
Pivovar Falkon
Žatec, Czech Republic
{ pivofalkon.cz }
MILK STOUT, 6.6%

After an afternoon spent in and around the hop-growing centre of Žatec, I was in the town's bustling brewpub/restaurant Pivovar U Orloje. A young man called Jakub, a brewer without a brewery, turned up, and several of us tasted his sweet stout. A sweet stout in the Czech Republic? The beer was equally serene, with chocolate truffles, milky coffee, and vanilla on the nose, which was repeated on the palate alongside a creamy and soothing mouthfeel, with dark malt rigor in the background keeping everything in order. Jakub is currently still making his beers in other people's breweries.

— *A train stop at Adlestrop* —

**GOVINDA CHEVALLIER EDITION**

Cheshire Brewhouse
Congleton, UK
{ cheshirebrewhouse.co.uk }
IPA, 6.8%

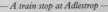

When Edward Thomas's train stopped at Adlestrop, and he wrote a poem inspired by this, it would have been comforting to think that a beer might have been close to hand. Perhaps he might have liked Govinda, as this English-style IPA is brewed with the barley strain Chevallier that was common in the late 19th and early 20th centuries. Made as a special, this is a muscular yet lustrous beer, with its juicy fruitiness acting in concord with the spice and pepper of the hop character alongside the dry graininess in the finish. Cheshire also matures some of it within oak.

— *The catcher of the rye* —

**ROGGEN ROLL ALE**

Schoppe Bräu
Berlin, Germany
{ schoppebraeu.de }
RYE BEER, 7%

This is a Roggenbier, a beer into which a certain amount of malted rye has been added, giving a dry, spicy, and crisp character; it's a style that skulks in the shadows of German beer, a speciality, a link with a tradition of rye-influenced beers that spreads from Germany across the Baltic states to Russia and Finland. Schoppe Bräu's version is a rich red beer with a caramel sweetness spreading across both aroma and flavor, which is also joined by a light dough-like sweetness, spiciness, nuttiness, and a crisp, dry finish. Drinking this takes you on a poetic journey across the north of Europe.

— *Pastoral poetry* —

**FARMER'S RESERVE**

Almanac Beer Company
San Francisco, CA, USA
{ almanacbeer.com }
SOUR BEER, 7%
(ABV VARIES)

The poetry of the seasons and the produce of the land are evoked by Almanac beers. Farmer's Reserve? It's part of a sequence called Farm to Barrel, and it's not just one beer, but different expressions, some made with various fruits picked locally (blackberry, strawberry, citrus), while there's an annual reserve that changes with the seasons, and there's also a Grand Cru. Expect varying degrees of fruitiness, tartness, dryness, complexity, and excitement, and let the poetry of the seasons run hand in hand with the beer.

*— The road less traveled —*

**TWILIGHT OF THE IDOLS**

Hill Farmstead Brewery

Greensboro, VT, USA

{ hillfarmstead.com }

PORTER, 7.5%

Poetry can be about travel, about the new places that inspire words. Those that idolize the beers of Hill Farmstead also travel, to the brewery's base in rural Vermont to buy bottles and growlers of Shaun Hill's peerless beers. Who knows what poetry is brought forth with each sip of this luscious and sensuous winter porter, infused with cinnamon, coffee, and vanilla? It's smooth, creamy, and roasty, dappled with chocolate and mocha coffee notes; it wears its cloak of cinnamon lightly, and finishes with a dry and bittersweet flourish.

*— Grace and complexity —*

**VIVEN IMPERIAL IPA**

Brouwerij van Viven
(brewed at De
Proefbrouwerij)
Sijsele, Belgium
{ viven.be }
IMPERIAL IPA, 8%

This beer might be big and potent, but there's a complexity about its aromatics and flavor that might be best suited to a poet like Seamus Heaney — you think you understand what's in your glass, and then something else gives you pause for thought. Dark golden in color, it has a bready, caramel-light nose with the caramel joining candy-store confection, citrus, and ripe soft fruit (apricot, banana), a hint of fresh pine, and a dry graininess that is followed by a keen and appetizing bitter finish. And that's just after the first reading (or should that be sip?).

"THE MOUTH OF A PERFECTLY
HAPPY MAN IS FILLED WITH
BEER."

ANCIENT EGYPTIAN PROVERB

*— Follow the lieder —*
### SCHÖNRAMER SAPHIR BOCK
Private Landbrauerei Schönram
Petting, Germany
{ brauerei-schoenram.de }
HELLER BOCK, 8%

"Bock," it says, and, for those who know the beer style, it's a surprise that this brew has eschewed the gloomy depths of darkness that traditional Bocks are inspired by. Instead, this Heller Bock gleams gold in the glass, the gold of the Nibelung perhaps. With the use of one single hop strain, the romantically named Saphir, Schönram's illustrious brewmaster Eric Toft has fashioned an eloquent poem of a beer, with soft lemon and honey notes on the nose (alongside a delicate breadiness), followed by an herbal, citrus-sweet, zingy, and honeyed character that makes this 8% beer all the more appetizing and drinkable.

*— Poetry that says please —*
### ZUNDERT TRAPPIST
Trappistenbrouwerij De Kievit
Zundert, the Netherlands
{ zunderttrappist.nl }
TRIPEL, 8%

Until 2013 there was only one Trappist brewery in the Netherlands, La Trappe, and then this luminous Tripel was released under the auspices of Cistercian monks at the Abdij Maria Toevlucht. The order's motto is "Pray and work," a way of life that neatly fits in the concept of brewing Trappist beers (which is not a style but an appellation), especially since you could argue that prayer is a form of poetry. The beer is copper-gold in color, with a blossoming nose of malt sweetness, candy sugar, and dried fruit such as raisins and banana chews, followed by similar notes on the palate, accompanied by a hefty alcoholic lift and a full-bodied texture.

— *Eloquent hop dream* —

## TAP5 MEINE HOPFENWEISSE

Schneider Weisse
Kelheim, Germany
{ schneider-weisse.de }
HOPFENWEISSE, 8.2%

In 2008, Schneider's Hopfenweisse became part of the brewery's portfolio, this time using Bavarian varieties Hallertauer Tradition and Saphir, with the result being a graceful and eloquent example of what hops can do when harnessed to the rich malt and wheat expression of a Weizenbock. It's fruity and peppery on the nose, melon with black pepper perhaps, or pineapple with coriander. It's then big and blowsy on the palate, alcoholic, fruity, and ripe, with a sweet background and a dry and bitter finish.

— *Loud and lyrical* —

## BORN TO DIE

BrewDog
Ellon, UK
{ brewdog.com }
IMPERIAL IPA, 8.5%

In the manner of a grand master or mistress of lyrical poetry who deigns to appear only twice a year at a literary festival of his or her choice, this rhapsodic, hop-laden double IPA also rations its appearances, being released in April and November. It's an intense and bracing experience of tropical fruit and pungent, savory hoppiness alongside a brisk, fast-talking carbonation; its name is a reference to the fact that it should be drunk within a month of purchase if you want to experience the vivid and vibrant freshness of its hop zinginess.

— *Brooding poem* —

## TONKA

Hawkshead Brewery
Staveley, UK
{ hawksheadbrewery.co.uk }
IMPERIAL PORTER, 8.5%

Breweries like to make Imperial porters. For this dark mahogany-colored poem in a glass, Hawkshead added tonka beans and cacao nibs, which take the beer into another sphere. There is plenty of coconut and vanilla on the nose, with more coconut, vanilla, and dark malts on the palate alongside an alcoholic booziness, vinous hints of cherry brandy, a chewy texture, and a dry, grainy finish. It is soft and soothing, slick and sensuous. This is a complex beer that one should study at great length as if it were an epic poem from the time of Homer.

— *Flemish heart* —
## TRIPEL
Six°North
Stonehaven, UK
{ sixdnorth.co.uk }
TRIPEL, 9%

❧

There's a harmony and gracefulness in the intriguing Belgian-style beers that Six°North brews. I first delved into the brewery's beers in Aberdeen, Scotland, where their bar is just around the corner from BrewDog's. It was there that I discovered this Tripel: gold in color, there is a distinctive pear-like note on the nose accompanied with a suggestion of ripe peach skin. On the palate, it's luscious and lustrous, with hints of banana and ripe peach, plus a trace of pepperiness in the background; the finish is honeyed and bittersweet. As I drank, I closed my eyes and imagined I was in Flanders.

— *With lines that sparkle* —
## DOMINUS VOBISCUM BRUT
Microbrasserie Charlevoix
Baie-Saint-Paul, Quebec, Canada
{ microbrasserie.com }
CHAMPAGNE BEER, 10%

❧

Champagne beers are the Noël Cowards of the beer world: urbane, silky, softly spoken, but still possessed of the occasional edge or acerbic turn of phrase that stops them being too bland. Seen as one of the most inventive breweries in Quebec's vibrant beer scene, Charlevoix have here produced a champagne beer that is a hazy yellow-gold in color, and topped by a lasting, fluffy head of white foam. The nose is suggestive of the acidity of champagne along with a hint of banana. In the mouth it has a Moussec-like blossom and the prickle of carbonation, alongside initial malt sweetness, citrus, more banana, and a gentle tartness; it finishes with a delicate fruitiness that brings back a slight suggestion of sweetness.

*— Holy orders —*

## ENGELSZELL GREGORIUS
## TRAPPISTENBIER

Stift Engelszell Trappistenbier-
Brauerei
Engelhartszell, Austria
{ stift-engelszell.at }
QUADRUPEL, 10.5%

There's a devotional aspect to brewing in a
Trappist abbey. Even though many (or most) of
the workers making the beer might be secular,
it would be hard for them to escape the
tranquillity and serenity of the monks,
especially as in most Trappist abbeys the
brothers are partial to the odd glass. That
spiritual and harmonious aspect can be
discovered in Trappist beers if you allow yourself for a moment to be lost in the whole magic
of beer being brewed in such an
environment (whatever your beliefs). When
I drank my first bottle of Gregorius in 2013, I
forgot for a few minutes that I was sitting in
a noisy craft beer bar in the "beer quarter" of
Rimini, Italy, and instead I studied and devoted
my time to the beer, whose taste was a rummy,
raisiny, burnt-sugar sweetness that was held
in check by burnt toasty notes. It was vinous,
alcoholic, chocolaty, leathery, and blessed
with a crystalline finish. My glass empty, I tuned
into the room again, wondering if I dared to
drink another.

*— A rhyme of time —*

## CUVEE DE TOMME

The Lost Abbey
San Marcos, CA, USA
{ lostabbey.com }
**WOOD-AGED SOUR, 11%**
**(ABV VARIES WITH VINTAGES)**

Time takes its toll with this magnificently endowed beer, an annual special that is named after its creator, Tomme Arthur, who is in charge of brewing at both The Lost Abbey and companion brewery Pizza Port. Time as in the time the initial brew of a dark, strong, Belgian-style brown ale spends in bourbon barrels in the company of sour cherries and Brettanomyces. A year elapses, and the beer is then bottled and ready to emerge into the world — and what a beer the world welcomes. The effect of time has produced a drink brimming with the brittle fruitiness of cherry, brushstrokes of vanilla and oak, sweet chimes of dark fruit and caramel, and the love of chocolate; oh, and there's also a tart tang of sourness somewhere in the embrace. There's more of this on the palate, with each sip revealing its deep complexity with a thirst-quenching tartness and an acidity that camouflages itself within the flurry of flavors, cunning and complete. Returning to time as our theme, this is also a beer that ages and advances with time. Buy two, drink one, and save the other for later.

SEVEN MOODS OF CRAFT BEER   POETIC

— *Love conquers* —
## EISENBAHN LUST
Cervejaria Sudbrack
Blumenau, Brazil
{ eisenbahn.com.br }
CHAMPAGNE BEER, 11.5%

Love poetry springs to mind when sipping this champagne beer (yes, sipping; this is a beer to take time over, rather like a missive to a loved one). Shakespeare's sonnets might be appropriate, or a work by Yeats, but given the beer's name something racier might spring to mind (John Donne perhaps). Dark bruised gold in color, and topped with a white head of foam, there's a sweetish and spicy nose, while sipping it brings forth its mouth-filling character as well as grainy, lychee, and grassy notes, and a finish that returns with a very light bowl of fruit. This is a unique attempt at those champagne beers that hesitantly emerged in Belgium in the 1990s, and as such should be constantly eulogized.

"O BEER! O HODGSON, GUINNESS, ALLSOPP, BASS! NAMES THAT SHOULD BE ON EVERY INFANT'S TONGUE."
CHARLES STUART CALVERLEY, 1862

WHEN YOU TASTE THESE BEERS, TRY TO
IMAGINE THE COUNTRY LIFE AND THE
RHYTHM OF THE PLOW THROUGH THE
SOIL. SAISONS ABOUND, AND THE RURAL
LIFE IS CONJURED, BUT THERE ARE
ALSO BEERS THAT HAVE BEEN BREWED
IN THE CITY THAT CAST A BUCOLIC
SPELL.

# BUCOLIC

### THE ANCHOR
Walberswick, Suffolk
{ anchoratwalberswick.com }

Sitting in the middle of the seaside village of Walberswick, The Anchor was built in the 1920s and is a classic example of what contemporary brewers called "Tudorbethan" — a sort of mock Tudor finish (steep gables, Elizabethan chimneys) bolted onto what was essentially a suburban house. Its landlord is a legendary figure of British beer, Mark Dorber, whose previous place, The White Horse, was arguably London's first craft beer pub. He carries on the good work at The Anchor with peerless ales from local brewery Adnams and a generous collection of global bottled beers.

### THE SALUTATION
Ham, Gloucestershire
{ the-sally-at-ham.com }

Back in early 2013, Peter Tiley left the rat race of London life and took up the helm of this traditional village pub, which had been serving locals since the 1840s (above). Since he started he's made it into a massive success, part of which is down to the interior — cozy bar, roaring fires in the winter, sunny pints outside in the verdant beer garden, pub games, and imaginative bar snacks. Beer became such a particular passion of Tiley that he installed his own microbrewery.

## THE BLUE BELL INN

Halkyn, North Wales

{ bluebell.uk.eu.org }

This is an old-fashioned, edge-of-village pub that started life as a pair of cottages in the 1700s. The village is close to the English border, and there are far-reaching views over the Wirral, Liverpool, and up along the northwest coast as far as Preston. On a summer's day, this makes for a stunning vista with a pint to hand. Landlord Steve Marquis has always prided himself on the number of beer varieties he has served since he took over the pub, with the figure hitting well over 1,000 toward the end of 2016.

## THE BHURTPORE

Aston, Cheshire

{ http://www.bhurtpore.co.uk }

This cozy village pub is a true temple of beer, offering up to 11 cask beers at any one time, alongside a selection of new-wave kegs as well as a bottled beer menu that wouldn't be out of place in a Belgian bar. For instance, if you want to contemplate a bottle of lambic from the venerable Cantillon of Brussels in the middle of the Cheshire countryside, then this is the place where you can get it.

## THE BEER HALL

Staveley, Cumbria

{hawksheadbrewery.co.uk }

When Hawkshead opened The Beer Hall in the small Lakes town of Staveley, it seemed like a bold attempt to redefine the space in which people drink beer. For a start, it's not a traditional pub; instead, the drinker is greeted by clean lines of design, minimal clutter, and the gleam of stainless steel. This is a bar, visitor center, beer shop, and beer kitchen all rolled into one, a place to enjoy great beer and food, especially Hawkshead's fabulous beers.

## ANDERSON

Fortrose, Scotland

{ theanderson.co.uk }

This is a former coaching inn and station hotel in a small country town, where the decor has the word "eclectic" stamped across its forehead: stag heads, beer and wine paraphernalia, original art, theater posters from obscure productions, candles stuck in bottles from unknown Dutch breweries. It is also a magnificent center for beer (and food), with nine draught beers and plenty of bottled Belgian beers, as well as others from around the world (Mikkeller's beers feature strongly as well). Every year the pub closes in November and reopens just before Christmas.

— *Urban pressure drop* —
### THROWBACK IPA
Pirate Life
Adelaide, Australia
{ piratelife.com.au }
SESSION IPA, 3.5%

— *A summer sense of sour* —
### THE BLEND
Wild Beer Co.
Westcombe, UK
{ wildbeerco.com }
BELGIAN-STYLE
GUEUZE, 4.7%

— *Spanish mountains* —
### TRIGA
Gisberga
Huesca, Spain
{ gisberga.com }
WHEAT BEER, 4.8%

IPA is an urban beer. It was born in London, brought up in Burton-on-Trent, and has more city berths than Airbnb. On the other hand, a session IPA can be considered a bucolic kind of beer style; it's a tranquil beer, a tilt away from city temptation, but it has enough hop aggression to suggest a farmer asking you to get off his land. Even though it's brewed in the city of Adelaide, you can imagine taking several cans of this rather inviting beer into the countryside. There's grapefruit, perhaps a hint of orange, on the nose, while the palate is refreshing, with more citrus, before its dry and bitter finish.

Hidden away in the hills of East Somerset, Wild Beer likes to experiment with various yeasts and let its beers rest in a variety of barrels. The Blend was first produced in summer 2015, when having reached its third birthday Wild Beer blended five of its beers, which had been fermented with different wild yeasts and aged for different amounts of time. The result was a magnificent beer, with a grapefruit-tinged spritziness on the palate, a counterpoint of sweet and sour, and citrus on the edge of ruin, all of which was enough to make the palate jump for joy. This is a beer to age.

Water tumbles down from the majestic high Spanish Pyrenees mountains to be eventually used in Gisberga's brewing process. The hard work then takes place in the brewery, and this delicate, farmhouse-styled wheat beer is the result. Straw-gold in color, veering toward dark orange, it's a light and refreshing beer, with a tang of citrus and a swipe of spice on both the nose and the palate. There's an appetizing acidity at loose as well, which helps give the beer an eminent presence on the dining table, or, with the Pyrenees in mind, a picnic would be more appropriate.

— *Modern fieldwork* —

## WORKER'S COMP SAISON

Two Roads Brewing
Stratford, CT, USA
{ tworoadsbrewing.com }
SAISON, 4.8%

The joy of a Saison is that it is a moveable feast, a brewing philosophy that each brewer has his or her own idea of. Some brewers add spices, others don't. Some hop it up, others turn it down. For Two Roads' Saison, brewmaster Phil Markowski uses a variety of grains (barley, wheat, rye, oats, spelt) alongside moderate hopping and a traditional Belgian farmhouse yeast strain to produce a beer bursting with tropical fruit notes on both nose and palate alongside a peppery and clove-like spiciness that results in a exceptionally refreshing beer.

— *Where elderflowers grow* —

## SAISON CAZEAU

Brasserie Cazeau
Templeuve, Belgium
{ brasseriedecazeau.be }
SAISON, 5%

The beer style Saison got its name from being seasonal, and Cazeau's interpretation of the style is just that. This Saison Cazeau can only be brewed over three weeks in May and June. The reason for this is that brewery founder Laurent Agache puts elderflowers in the brew, which grow on his own land and are available only during this short period. They are cut in the morning, and then put in at the end of the boil.

The result is a luminous, light-gold beer, with notes of elderflower on the nose. There is a creamy mouthfeel, more elderflower fruitiness, and a sharp, tart finish.

— *Languid* —

## HYUGANATSU LAGER

Hideji Beer Brewery
Nobeoka, Japan
{ hideji-beer.jp }
FRUIT-FLAVORED
LAGER, 5%

You might want to imagine a summer's day, light fluffy clouds lazily drifting across a pale blue sky, while the sun's rays gently stroke the earth. This is the kind of day this crisp fruit-flavored lager was made for. Hyuganatsu is added to the mix, a citrus fruit whose taste is close to yuzu. Its presence in this award-winning beer imparts a rich burst of orange-like citrus alongside a hint of mid-palate acidity that makes the beer all the more refreshing. And while the summer afternoon stretches out with all the languorous ease of a cat, let this beer be your bucolic companion.

— *Beervana rusticity* —

### BIÈRE DE GARDE

Commons Brewery
Portland, OR, USA
{ commonsbrewery.com }
BIÈRE DE GARDE, 5.3%

You will find Commons
Brewery on a corner in
Portland, Oregon, a city that
is a far cry from the rustic
brewing traditions of *bière
de garde*. On the other hand,
*bière de garde* has always
been a moveable feast (some
are blond, some are amber,
some more hoppy, some more
malty). Portland's version is
definitely rustic, reminiscent
of the fields and villages of
the Pas-de-Calais region. It is
amber in color, and boisterous
on the nose with citrus, spice,
and the umami of yeast, while
sip after sip brings in more
citrus, spice, bittersweet malt,
and a lasting, dry finish.

— *A self-sufficient saison* —

### SAISON

Hof Ten Dormaal
Haacht, Belgium
{ hoftendormaal.com }
SAISON, 5.5%

Hof Ten Dormaal's beers
are brewed on a farm in the
middle of the countryside
north of Leuven in Belgium.
It's a farm with its own fields of
barley and hops, thus ensuring
the brewery is self-sufficient,
and that the only raw material
brought in is the yeast. This
Flemish Saison is pale and
winsome in the glass, with
aromatic notes of lemon-
flavored boiled sweets and a
hint of spicy coriander. On the
palate, there is a fine balance
between austerity and fatness,
while the brisk carbonation,
mid-palate pepperiness, a
slight hint of sourness, and
a long, dry finish add to the
complexity of the beer.

— *An idyll in a glass* —

### SAISON DE DOTTIGNIES

Brouwerij De Ranke
Dottignies, Belgium
{ www.deranke.be }
SAISON, 5.5%

Saison de Dottignies started
as a one-off beer called Hop
Flower Power, which was
brewed to celebrate
De Ranke's 15th anniversary
in 2009. A year later, the same
beer was tweaked to create
this perky Saison. Amber in
the glass, with a creamy head,
it's a spicy, briskly
carbonated beer, with a
Moussec-like mouthfeel.
It's fresh and flowery, citrusy,
and honeyed, and the
peppery spiciness is delicate.
De Ranke is best known for
its bitter XXX, but with this
beer the brewery's founders,
Nino Bacelle and Guido Devos,
demonstrated that they could
summon up the rural idyll that
we expect from a Saison.

— *Blended bucolicity* —
## SAISON
Casey Brewing &
Blending
Glenwood Springs,
CO, USA
{ caseybrewing.com }
SAISON, 5.5%

The name says it all. At the
start, Troy Casey oversees
the first stage of a brew in a
neighboring brewery, and the
unfermented wort is brought
back to his barrel cellar, where
fermentation takes place in
oak barrels with added yeast,
including wild strains. After
several months, the blending
of various beers takes place.
Saison was the first beer
Casey made and he says, "It
defines everything we are as
a brewery." The beer is tart,
thirst-quenching, sprightly in
its carbonation, lemony, spicy,
and crisp in the finish.

— *A San Diego farmhouse* —
## LOMALAND
Modern Times Beer
San Diego, CA, USA
{ moderntimesbeer.com }
SAISON, 5.5%

The beer style of the Wallonian
country gets an outing in San
Diego, and amid the blaring of
car horns on freeways and the
hustle and bustle of the city,
this bright-yellow hazy beer
brings a calmness that
transports the drinker to
that lonely farmhouse where
Saison has been made for
generations. On the nose there
is white pepper, plus hints of
banana (think Bavarian Weiss
banana) and orange. There's
a big mouthfeel, Moussec-like
in its elegance, with peppery
spice and lemon citrus
floating in mid-palate, moving
on to a dry finish that suggests
another swig might well be
in order.

— *Stout du Rhône* —
## VIELLE BRUNE
Brasserie Thiriez
Esquelbecq, France
{ brasseriethiriez.com }
STOUT, 5.8%

Once a year, Raymond Thiriez
brews a thick, dark stout,
and then leaves it in Côtes du
Rhône oak barrels for anything
up to six months. The result is
this complex and vinous beer
that is the color of the darkest
night you could imagine. It
has licorice, oak, caramel, and
hints of berries on the nose,
while once sipped it's hard
not to continue enjoying its
vinous, gently tart, moderately
sweet presence on the tongue,
while it proceeds to a dry
finish that keeps the chimes of
a delicate sweetness ringing
away as you prepare yourself
for the next sip.

SEVEN MOODS OF CRAFT BEER    BUCOLIC

— *La Traviata in a field* —
### NUOVA MATTINA
Birrificio del Ducato
Busseto, Italy
{ birrificiodelducato.it }
SAISON, 5.8%

Former home-brewer
Giovanni Campari started
del Ducato in 2007 in Verdi's
home village of La Roncole,
a fact he celebrated with the
much-awarded Verdi Imperial
stout. Nuova Mattina, or New
Morning, is a less muscular
soul than the stout. Pouring
a hazy golden orange, this is
a peppery, flinty, dry Saison
that has ginger, coriander,
green pepper, and chamomile
in its make-up. There's soft
carbonation, a boiled-sweet
fruitiness, a tartness, an
esoteric, otherworldly
spiciness, the hint of lemon,
and a big, dry finish. At once
it's light, complex, and
refreshing — an aria of a beer.

— *Sunny beer-light* —
### SOLSTICE D'ÉTÉ AUX
### FRAMBOISES
Brasserie Dieu du Ciel!
Saint-Jérôme, Canada
{ dieuduciel.com }
FRUIT BEER, 5.9%

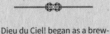

Dieu du Ciel! began as a brewpub in Montreal in 1998, and
soon developed a reputation
for its intriguing mix of beers.
Solstice d'Été was the
brainwave of head brewer
Jean-François Gravel, who was
a big fan of fruity sour beers
and lambics. His aim was
to create a sour fruit beer in
which the fruit was fermented
instead of added at the end;
there would also be no
artificial flavorings. The result
is this thirst-quencher in which
the fruitiness of the
raspberries merges with
tartness and light acidity. As
the name suggests, an ideal
beer to drink in the sun.

— *An allotment* —
### SIBERIA
Ilkley Brewery
Ilkley, UK
{ ilkleybrewery.co.uk }
SAISON, 5.9%

The inclusion of rhubarb
in this earthy, spicy, and
refreshing straw gold-colored
Belgian-style Saison is a
triumph. First brewed in
2012 using locally grown
rhubarb, there's a flurry of
light lemon, smooth vanilla,
and peppery spice notes on
the nose (vanilla and grains of
paradise are added), while the
taste is a fusion of tart apple,
honeyed sweetness, rhubarb
tartness, and a light citrus-like
undercurrent. The finish is dry
and bitter. Unsurprisingly, this
Yorkshire-based brewery
suggests a bottle of Siberia
would be a wonderful
companion to a panna cotta
with rhubarb compote.

*— It's a long way from Wallonia —*

## ICHIGO ICHIE

Kyoto Brewing Company

Kyoto, Japan

{ kyotobrewing.com }

SAISON, 5.9%

The name of this beer translates as "each moment only once," a train of thought connected to the Japanese tea ceremony, the idea that you put everything into the moment, as that moment might never come again. Following on from that, it's probably a good idea to keep this approach in mind when drinking this orange-gold Saison: appreciating the drink and the work that has gone into creating it — a beer that is so far from its home territory of Wallonia. It's peppery and spicy in the classic Saison style, but mid-palate splashes of citrus and tropical fruit add their own gustatory joy before it finishes dry and bracing.

*— A gardening beer —*

## VI WHEAT, 6%

Brasserie de Jandrain-Jandrenouille

Jandrain-Jandrenouille, Belgium

{ brasseriedejandrainjandrenouille.com }

WHEAT ALE, 6%

This is a small brewery, and the two brewers who set it up have day jobs with a hop company. In this hazy orange wheat ale, the hops are quiet, like sleepy children, with the aromatics bringing a delicate, orange-like note alongside a tartness. It is mid-bodied in its mouthfeel, and there is the ghost of an orange. However, what really defines it as an exceptional beer is its refreshing quality, its ability to awaken the palate with a combination of earthiness, sweetness, and pepperiness. It's the kind of beer you want to drink after, say, mowing the lawn, but at 6% strength, you might want your gardener to do it instead as you watch.

— *Borderland brew* —

### SAISON D'EPEAUTRE

Brasserie de Blaugies
Dour, Belgium
{ brasseriedeblaugies.com }
SAISON, 6%

This family-run brewery is based in a small village called Dour, which is just a stone's throw from the French border. This is rich farming country with a gently undulating landscape, an ideal accompaniment to the Saison d'Epeautre. There is a hint of a Brettanomyces-like earthiness on the nose, conjoined with a hop-derived citrusiness, while sips reveal sharp grapefruit notes and a tartness on the palate; the use of the ancient grain spelt in the mash adds a cake-like backdrop to the palate. This is a classic Saison, a beer that takes the drinker to the heart of the traditions of this sublime beer style.

— *Pastoral does punk* —

### FARMHOUSE IPA

Lervig Aktiebryggeri
Stavanger, Norway
{ lervig.no }
IPA, 6%

This is a thoroughbred of a collaboration between Lervig and Yorkshire brewery Magic Rock, resulting in a cross between an IPA — with bright colorful hopping, courtesy of Citra and Centennial — and a Saison, featuring a mixture of Saison yeast and Brettanomyces. The result is an explosion of flavor with a sashay of tropical fruit on the nose and palate when the beer is young, but as it ages, the Brettanomyces adds its own character to the beer, muting the fruit, and creating an earthy, dry, spicy character. This is a beer with two sides to its personality, depending on what age you drink it.

— *Layer cake* —

### FARMHOUSE RED

La Sirène Brewing
Melbourne, Australia
{ lasirene.com.au }
FLEMISH-STYLE RED
ALE, 6%

La Sirène has been influenced by the rustic brewing traditions of northern France and Belgium, and this Flemish-style red ale is a good example. As well as the use of five different speciality malts, fresh rose buds, hibiscus, and dandelions are also added. The result is a chestnut-red-colored beer with a fine head of creamy foam; a ripe, plummy fruitiness alongside the delicate waft of rose dominates the aroma; while sip after sip reveals layers of tartness, creaminess, vinousness, a hint of toasty caramel, and more stone fruit (cherry, plum) before it finishes dry and appetizing.

— *Rock star* —
## TROLLTUNGA GOOSEBERRY SOUR IPA
Buxton Brewery
Buxton, UK
{ buxtonbrewery.co.uk }
IPA, 6.3%

This is pale golden with a creamy head, beneath which bubbles rise. There is an initial waft of lychee, a ringing chime of tropical fruitiness; then the aroma transforms itself to an approximation of the perfumy, grape-like lightness of Riesling. Juicy and tart at the front of the palate, with a juiciness and tartness in the finish, as well as a slight puckering of sourness; in the middle there are gooseberry and grapefruit, a light and lithe touch, and even the suggestion of a peppery spiciness. With gooseberries, hops, and sourness, this Buxton-Lervig collaboration is named after a Norwegian rock and is the next best thing to being out there.

— *The grate outdoors* —
## SIWY MIŚ
Browar Widawa
Chrząstawa Mała,
Poland
GRODZISKIE, 6.2%

Imagine a campfire, gentle smoke fumes drifting on the air, that, along with the open air, helps to stimulate the appetite. Now pour a glass of this beer, a grodziskie, a revival of a Polish beer style that has smoked wheat in the mix (at 6.2% this is almost twice as strong as grodziskie's traditional strength). On the nose, there's that campfire, not too heady, and a hint of smoke-cured cheese perhaps. The beer is a hazy orange color, with a bracing but soothing swoon of smoke on the palate, alongside a malty sweetness and a hint of tartness before it finishes dry.

"OH I HAVE BEEN TO LUDLOW
FAIR, AND LEFT MY NECKTIE
GOD KNOWS WHERE, AND
CARRIED HALF WAY HOME, OR
NEAR, PINTS AND QUARTS OF
LUDLOW BEER."
A. E. HOUSMAN, *A SHROPSHIRE LAD*,
1896

*— Et in Arcadia ego —*
### GUEUZE TILQUIN À L'ANCIENNE
Gueuzerie Tilquin
Bierghes, Belgium
{ gueuzerietilquin.be }
GUEUZE, 6.4%

Musty, sweet, earthy, in possession of a champagne-like spritziness, or maybe it's grapefruit: all these qualities combine to produce a thirst-quenching and refreshing beer, a beer the color of a hazy sunset, a beer that emerges from the Wallonian countryside (a rarity — Gueuze is associated with Flanders, and this is the only one coming from the other part of Belgium). This is also a beer that is not brewed in the actual sense of the word, being instead a blend of one-, two-, and three-year-old lambics coming from four different suppliers—Boon, Lindemans, Giradin, and Cantillon—which are fermented and matured in Tilquin's own facilities. According to Pierre Tilquin, who founded this Gueuzerie (or blender) in 2009, this blend of lambics from different producers has the advantage of giving his beer a more complete taste, "and I hope, more accessible." It is a fabulous beer, the sort of beer that you drink and think, *"Et in Arcadia ego."*

— *Fields of gold* —

**PIER**

Trillium Brewing

Boston, MA, USA

{ trilliumbrewing.com }

WHEAT ALE, 6.4%

There are wheat beers, both Belgian and Bavarian, and then there is wheat ale, a beer style that emerged during the US craft beer revolution of the 1980s. Trillium, which was founded in 2013, has taken the style, added a lush trio of hops (Galaxy, Citra, Columbus), and come up with a refreshing gold-colored beer whose nose resonates with tingling tropical fruits, while its creamy mouthfeel provides a luscious background for both tropical fruit and citrus to jingle-jangle away. The finish is dry and crisp, and lingers like the bittersweet memories of a lost love affair.

— *Jasmine and hibiscus* —

**RED SKY**

Shenanigans Brewing

Sydney, Australia

{ shenanigansbrewing.com }

IPA, 6.5%

Gypsy brewing can be such a frolic—just ask Shenanigans, who have been brewing small batches of their beers in and around Sydney since 2014. Their declared aim is to make beers that they would like to drink themselves, beers that are both approachable and interesting for beer aficionados. Red Sky is such a beer, a left-field take on the classic US IPA that also has jasmine and hibiscus flowers in the mix. The result is an amber-colored joy, with hop-derived floral notes merging with the jasmine and hibiscus on the nose, and plenty of citrus and tropical fruit on the palate alongside a tartness and a big bitterness in the finish.

— *Wallonia's star* —

## SAISON DUPONT

Brasserie Dupont

Tourpes, Belgium

{ brasserie-dupont.com }

SAISON, 6.5%

Saison is a style of beer that has its roots in the farmhouse ales of the Hainaut province of Wallonia, the French-speaking part of Belgium. This is a rich agricultural land and, until World War II, many farms in the area would have brewed beers for their workers, making use of whatever grains were available (barley, wheat, rye) along with various herbs and spices, especially if there was a shortage of hops. Saison Dupont is the Saison that defines the style for many, and is brewed on a former farm that has been in the same family since the 1920s. Dark gold in color, it's an austere and spicy Saison (although no spices are used), with resiny notes on the nose. On the palate, its sweetness is restrained, and there's a Moussec-like mouthfeel before a dry finish that resonates with additional hints of spice. This is a beer with a sense of its own place in the land.

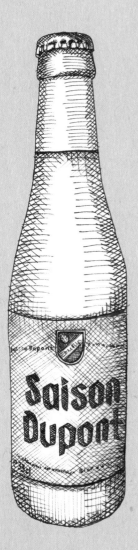

— *Nordic season* —
## SAISON
Nøgne ø
Grimstad, Norway
{ nogne-o.com }
SAISON, 6.5%

This is a Nordic Saison, brewed close to the southern coast of Norway in a landscape of forests and lakes. Orange sweetness, orange peel, the herbal spiciness of cough drops, hints of cooked banana plus white pepper: this all sounds like a recipe for disaster, but it works. It's hazy and it's yellow gold, initially with a large snow-white head of foam. This is a generous Saison, flinty but also fruity, full bodied, spicy, suggestive of caraway seed and aniseed, some orange, and a mid-palate puff of tartness. The finish is dry and lasting, with a high note of spice and a low growl of bitterness.

— *Time* —
## SAISON À LA PROVISION
Burning Sky
Firle, UK
{ burningskybeer.com }
SAISON, 6.5%

Formerly head brewer at Dark Star, Mark Tranter set up Burning Sky in 2013 in a small village in rural Sussex, England. To him, nature and the landscape are as much an inspiration as the beers he tastes on his travels and the experience he gained at Dark Star. Time is an important ingredient in Burning Sky's brewing philosophy, as the growing number of barrels demonstrates. This lean and fruity Saison is evidence of this, spending several months slumbering in an oak barrel with added lactobacillus and Brettanomyces. The result is a refreshing beer.

— *City parklife* —
## DELTA IPA
Brussels Beer Project
Brussels, Belgium
{ beerproject.be }
IPA, 6.5%

According to the label, this is a Saison IPA. There's plenty of hop zap and zest, but there's a peppery spicy element that throws intriguing shapes in the glass. There's a chive-like note allied with orange sweetness on the nose, plus a hint of herbal (think cough drops) in the background. There's brisk carbonation, a dryness, and mid-palate juiciness of tropical fruits. It's flinty and crystalline, dry and crisp, fruity and fastidious in its attention on the palate; the bitterness is lasting and lingering in the finish; there's a lasting dryness as well. Sit back and consider, and let the sounds of the city fade away.

— *Fenland magic* —

## COOLSHIP

Elgoods

Wisbech, UK

{ elgoods-brewery.co.uk }

**LAMBIC STYLE, 6.7%**

Elgoods is the quintessential English family brewery, quietly getting on with brewing bitters and golden ales, and supplying its own pubs and the wider trade. However, in 2013 it found itself setting off in an entirely different direction with a new beer named Coolship. The beer came about when an American visitor noticed two unused coolers that, as the name suggests, were once utilized to cool the hopped wort after the boil. Why not make a lambic, suggested the visitor, which, after careful research, Elgoods' head brewer Alan Pateman went on to do. The result was this enigmatic beer that owes more to the de la Senne valley outside Brussels than its home region of the English Fens. Copper in color, it has an earthy nose with hints of sherry, grapefruit sweetness, and English mustard. Tart and softly acidic on first taste, more sips reveal a grapefruit-like tartness, a soft sweetness in the background, and more hints of sherry. They say you cannot teach an old dog new tricks, but in this case Elgoods (whose symbol is a black dog) proved that to be wrong.

— *Hop heroics* —
### HARVEST
Sierra Nevada Brewing
Chico, CA, USA
{ sierranevada.com }
**IPA, 6.7%**

Harvest is a series of IPAs released every year, an experiment with hops, and a sign of the seriousness that Sierra Nevada takes in pursuing flavor and aroma. Some years there are four in the series, others five. One beer will feature a single hop, another an experimental strain that might not even have a name; another will be a showcase for "wet" or "green" hops, which go straight from the bine to the brewery in a matter of hours. There might also be a beer that features hops from the southern hemisphere, which enables Sierra Nevada to feature hops from two harvests a year. Whatever the configuration, these will be beers with a blast of fresh hop aromatics, and plenty of fruit on the palate.

— *Urban farmhouse* —
### STATESIDE SAISON
Stillwater Artisanal
Baltimore, MD, USA
{ stillwater-artisanal.com }
**SAISON, 6.8%**

"American farmhouse ale," it says on the label, bringing forth images of Stateside Saison being brewed on a farm somewhere in the countryside. The reality is very different. Founded by onetime Electronica DJ Brian Strumke, Stillwater is very much a gypsy brewery, with various breweries around the world providing a space where its eclectic range of beers (many with the prefix "American Farmhouse Ales") can be brewed. This is a classic nod to the Wallonian Saison, though with the addition of US and New Zealand hops, which give it a zest and a zip of fruitiness. The beer is orange-yellow in the glass, spicy and peppery, dry and fruity, and the finish lingers like the echo of thunder in the hills.

— *Bohemian rhapsody* —
### SAISON
Pivovar Matuška
Broumy, Czech
Republic
{ pivovarmatuska.cz }
SAISON, 6.8%

Here is a rare treat, the classic Wallonian farmhouse ale brewed in a small Czech village to the southwest of Prague, a family brewery, which has gained plaudits for its beers across Europe and the United States (where both father Martin Matuška and son Adam have judged in prestigious competitions). It's a sign of how international the Saison style has become, and yet it still manages to retain its rural connections, as anyone drinking this golden ale with its flurry of oranges and lemons, leather and spice on the nose will concur.

— *Flemish cheek* —
### SAISON D'ERPE-MERE
Brouwerij De Glazen
Toren
Erpe-Mere, Belgium
{ glazentoren.be }
SAISON, 6.9%

Saisons are normally brewed in the French-speaking parts of Belgium rather than in East Flanders, but Jeff van den Steen, Dirk de Pauw, and Mark de Neef had other ideas when they set up Glazen Toren in 2004. Saison d'Erpe-Mere was their debut beer, and the first-ever Flemish example of this style. It has lemon on the nose, with an undertow of a Burgundy-like earthiness along with a hint of sweet spice. The palate is bittersweet, with more citrus fruit plus a hint of white pepper; the mouthfeel is slightly champagne-like before it all cascades into a thirst-quenching finish.

— *Travel by beer* —
### SAISON
Extraomnes
Marnate, Italy
{ extraomnes.com }
SAISON, 6.9%

Based in the small town of Marnate, a few miles north-west of Milan, Extraomnes is often seen as one of the top craft breweries in Italy. Founded by Luigi "Schigi" d'Amelio in 2010, the brewery's beers are inspired by Belgian brewing traditions, which is why we have this Saison. Hazy gold in color, it has the traditional Saison-style aromatics of peppery spiciness with hints of citrus in the background. It is grainy, grassy, citrusy, and dry on the palate, with a lasting finish. We often talk about a beer transporting the drinker somewhere else; in the case of Extraomnes, it's to the fields of Wallonia.

— *The landscape of desire* —

**DEVIL'S REST**

Burning Sky

Firle, UK

{ burningskybeer.com }

IPA, 7%

As well as being a rugged IPA, Devil's Rest is a place on the Sussex Downs, not far from Firle in England. As well as the brewing influences of the US and Belgium, landscape is also influential in the way Burning Sky's founder and brewer, Mark Tranter, approaches his beers: "This is an area I love and every beer I have thought about was while yomping around the Downs." There's a great contrast between the calm bucolic surroundings and influences that direct Tranter and the urban-like IPA-ness of Devil's Rest. Almost red in color, it has a fragrant cherry/cedar nose (with a hint of amaretto), a nutty, stone-like center, sensual citrus, and a ferocious dry finish. It's the kind of beer that straddles town and country and creates its own landscape.

— *Electric country* —

**8 WIRED SAISON SAUVIN**

8 Wired

Warkworth, New Zealand

{ 8wired.co.nz }

SAISON, 7%

No. 8 wire is the specific gauge of wire that is used throughout New Zealand, but 8 Wired is also the name of the brewery set up by Søren Eriksen in 2009 while he was still working with Renaissance brewery in Blenheim, South Island. 8 Wired, based in the North Island, produces an eclectic range of beers, including this harmonic take on the farmhouse ales of Wallonia. Intense draughts of passion fruit and ripe peach emerge from the glass, while the palate is dry and juicy, with tropical fruitiness alongside a peppery assertiveness. The finish is dry and lasting.

> "A FINE BEER MAY BE JUDGED WITH ONE SIP, BUT IT'S BETTER TO BE THOROUGHLY SURE."
>
> CZECH PROVERB

*— Strange fruit —*
### FARMHOUSE ALE BUTIÂ
Cervejaria Way
Pinhais, Brazil
{ waybeer.com.br }
SAISON, 7.2%

Way has come a long way since Alessandro Oliveira and Alejandro Winocur launched the brewery in 2010. Based in the southern state of Paraná, Way's ambition was to bring North American craft beer culture to southern Brazil. Brewed in collaboration with Brian Strumke of Stillwater, this beer is an herbal and spicy Saison with the addition of the Brazilian fruit butiá. The result is a tart and quenching beer with a delicate fruitiness reminiscent of maybe pineapple and banana whispering away in the background, while the addition of Brettanomyces in the bottle adds an earthy note.

*— Orchard moonlight —*
### SORIACHI ACE
Brooklyn Brewery
New York, NY, USA
{ brooklynbrewery.com }
SAISON, 7.2%

Soriachi Ace is a hop variety developed in Japan in the 1970s that languished in obscurity until 2009 when Brooklyn used it for this Saison. At the same time, the variety was being grown in the United States, and it has gone on to become a big favorite with home-grown craft breweries. Brooklyn's trailblazer is a good example of the complexity this hop brings to the beer, as luminous notes of lemon peel and lemongrass leap out of the glass, and continue on the palate alongside black pepper, mellow honey, and a suggestion of pear. The finish is dry and long, resonant with more lemongrass and spice.

*— Sense of somewhere else —*
### NORWEGIAN FARMHOUSE
Poppyland
Cromer, UK
{ www.poppylandbeer.com }
FARMHOUSE ALE, 7.4%

Poppyland is a one-man-band, the passion of Martin Warren, a geologist and former museum curator who combs the Norfolk countryside, foraging for intriguing ingredients. For Norwegian Farmhouse, he crossed the North Sea to Norway to investigate a traditional beer called Vossaøl, and returned with a special strain of yeast. He then added juniper he'd collected, and the result is this dark red beer with a rich earthy and roasty nose. On the palate it has a soft mouthfeel (traditionally Vossaøl is low in carbonation) with fruitcake notes followed by a long, bitter finish.

— *Remembrance day* —
### EVERETT
Hill Farmstead
Greensboro, VT, USA
{ hillfarmstead.com }
PORTER, 7.5%

Is this the best brewery in the world? Are these the best beers in the world? Superlatives fly about with the abandonment of mayflies on a sunstruck summer river when it comes to discussing Hill Farmstead. Hidden away in the green lush countryside of Vermont, close to the small town of Greensboro, this is a brewery that sees crowds of fans descend on it whenever its retail shop is open: growlers are filled, and tailgates groan beneath the weight of cases. However, these are beers that deserve their plaudits, as does Shaun Hill's approach toward his craft — there is an intense search for flavor. There are sours, IPAs, wood-aged beers, and easy-drinking beers that all pulsate with flavor.

Then there is what Hill calls the "Ancestral series," beers that are named after long-gone forebears (the brewery is on land that has been owned by the family for generations). Everett is named for his grandfather's brother, and it is a smooth and silky porter languid with chocolate, coffee, and vanilla both on the nose and in the taste. The finish has bitterness and roastiness, counterpointed by the silkiness of chocolate and coffee.

*— Bringing it back home (nearly) —*
## MONT DES CATS
Abbaye Mont Des Cats
Godewaersvelde, France
(brewed in Belgium)
{ abbaye-montdescats.com }
BELGIAN STRONG ALE, 7.6%

The Trappist monks of the Abbaye Mont Des Cats, which is located in Godewaersvelde on the French-Belgian border near the coast, used to brew their own beer until the brewery was destroyed during World War I. In 2011 they decided to resurrect the old tradition, but as they had no brewery they turned to Chimay in Belgium. The result is this copper-colored beer. The nose has a caramel sweetness that links arms with hints of fruitcake and banana, while it's medium sweet on the palate, with plenty of ripe fruit, caramel, toffee, and a maltiness suggestive of toasted grains. This is a smooth and fruity beer that induces a monk-like sense of serenity in the drinker.

*— Winter warmer —*
## SNOWBALL SAISON
To Øl
Copenhagen, Denmark
{ to-ol.dk }
SAISON, 8%

For the two guys behind To Øl, being a gypsy brewery is a way of life, a way of maintaining their curiosity and making beers that are out of the ordinary (although they have a brewpub in Copenhagen, which is also home to their barrel-aging facility). Snowball Saison was originally conceived — as the name might suggest — for the winter season, a classic riff on this most rural of beer styles. It has a dry and crisp-in-the-mouth feel, with a lingering tartness (thanks to the addition of Brettanomyces); there is spice, pepperiness, citrus, and hints of pineapple, while the finish is livened up with a bracing bitterness.

*— Here is Eden —*
## PLINY THE ELDER
Russian River Brewing
Santa Rosa, CA, USA
{ russianriverbrewing.com }
### IMPERIAL IPA, 8%

Is Pliny The Elder a cult beer? It could be. This zealously hopped Imperial IPA is a beer that is primed for hardened hop-heads and pined over by those on the other side of the world to whom it is mysterious and magical. It is a beer that is about the wholesome honesty of hops, the freshness, the tangy, orangey, resiny, pungent aromatics, and the flavors of hops. The Sonoma Valley is where it comes from, where grapes grow and there is now a vibrant beer scene. You have to applaud the ingenuity of Vinnie Cilurzo, who developed the first Imperial IPA at the brewery Blind Pig; you have to applaud the foresight with which he wondered what would happen if he did this and then that. And when he started Russian River he continued the process, and the result is Pliny, a beer that Russian River advise its devotees to drink fresh, so it's worth a trip to this Eden-like part of the world in order to drink a beer that defines a style.

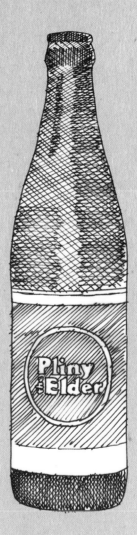

SEVEN MOODS OF CRAFT BEER

*— Tranquilly Trappist —*
### TRIPEL BIRRA TRAPPISTA ITALIANA
Abbazia delle Tre Fontane
Rome, Italy
{ abbaziatrefontane.it }
TRIPEL, 8.5%

In 2015 Italy had its first Trappist brewery when the monks at Rome's Abbazia delle Tre Fontane ("abbey of three fountains") added a beer to the list of products they make at the monastery. You have to imagine the contemplative silence as the beer is brewed, a silence that is transferred to the beer when it is poured into the glass, a harbinger of tranquillity and an ethereal taste. Golden-orange in color, it has a sweet citrus tanginess on the nose, alongside flurries of spiciness. It's creamy and spicy on the palate (eucalyptus is added to the mix), medium-bodied, peppery, bittersweet and light, and mineral-like in the finish.

*— An Orange County orator —*
### SAISON RUE
Bruery Terraux
Anaheim, CA, USA
{ brueryterreux.com }
SAISON, 8.5%

Bruery Terraux is the name given to the taproom and brewing playground for The Bruery, which is a separate facility for this brewing star of Orange County. In this place, wild and sour beers are conceived and drunk, with Saison Rue, originally produced in the main brewery a few miles away, now finding its home here. This scintillating beer is conceived in the very best traditions of Wallonian farmhouse brewing, with wild yeast and rye adding to its complexity. Orange-amber in color, it has citrus and spice on the nose, while the palate sparkles with more spice, pepperiness, citrus, an earthiness from the wild yeast, and a creaminess from the rye. The finish is dry and appetizingly bitter.

— *Rustic in a glass* —
## ABBAYE DE SAINT BON-CHIEN
Brasserie des Franches-Montagnes
Saignelégier, Switzerland
{ brasseriebfm.ch }
WOOD-AGED BEER, 11%

Better known as BFM, this brewery is one of the pioneers of craft brewing in Switzerland, where light-colored lagers have long been the mainstay (and in some respects still are) of its beer culture; but things are changing. BFM began its journey in the rural village of Saignelégier in 1997, while this incredibly complex, wood-aged beer was first brewed in 2004 — it has been made annually ever since. It's a beer that is soured during the brewing process, and then aged in ancient wine oak casks for a year. The fruits of this repose are then blended to produce a beer of utmost complexity, that is reminiscent of a Flemish Oud Bru but, thanks to the various casks, it also has a vinous, port-like quality.

BREWERS' HEARTS AND MINDS
RUN WILD AND FREE WHEN IT
COMES TO THESE BEERS: SOME ADD
INGREDIENTS THAT GO AGAINST
THE GRAIN; OTHERS LET THEIR
IMAGINATIONS TAKE UP FANCIFUL
IDEAS AND PRODUCE MAGIC. LET
YOUR MIND DO THE SAME.

# IMAGINATIVE

# INTERNATIONAL COMPETITIONS

## THE GREAT BRITISH BEER FESTIVAL

{ gbbf.org.uk }

On the morning of the start of the Great British Beer Festival in early August, invited judges gather to sample a variety of cask beers, all of them with one aim: to choose the winners of the Campaign for Real Ale's Champion Beers of Britain (above). As in many competitions, all the beers are grouped into style categories, with the judges sipping and speculating through the morning before choosing the winners. The ultimate accolade is the Champion Beer of Britain, an award that can significantly boost a brewery's sales and profile. Until 2016, the awards were announced from a stage at the so-called trade session on the opening afternoon, but that year CAMRA decided to hold a gala dinner with the winners being announced then.

## BRUSSELS BEER CHALLENGE

{ brusselsbeerchallenge.com }

Although there had been beer competitions in Belgium before, it wasn't until the Brussels Beer Challenge started in 2012 that it was felt that one of the great brewing countries of Europe had the competition it deserved. Judges come from all over the world to spend three morning sessions evaluating up to 35 beers each day. Despite its name, the competition has been held in Liège, Leuven, Antwerp, and Brussels. In Brussels, the city's magnificent-looking Stock Exchange is used as the venue for nearly 80 judges. Unlike the Great American and British Beer Festivals' competitions, entries for the Challenge come from breweries around the world, and this often provokes soul-searching in Belgium's media if there are fewer Belgian award winners than from the US or Italy.

## INTERNATIONAL BREWING AWARDS

{ brewingawards.org }

This is the oldest brewing competition in the world, first held at the Brewers' National Exhibition and Market in 1888, which was then an annual event in London, England. It then returned in 1890, but it wasn't until 1901 that it became an annual fixture, subsequently interrupted only by two world wars. The competition is different from most others held around the world, as it is judged by professional brewers only (although Michael Jackson was called on to judge when the organizers needed help on the new speciality beers coming in from Europe). After being held at various other venues in London, Birmingham, and Munich, and the demise of the exhibition, it is now held every two years in the home of British beer, Burton-on-Trent.

## THE GREAT AMERICAN BEER FESTIVAL

{ greatamericanbeerfestival.com }

Judges (brewers, journalists, brewing industry professionals) travel from all over the world to evaluate the hundreds of beers offered for their consideration when the Great American Beer Festival opens in Denver, Colorado, at the start of October (above). There are 96 style categories (with some further divided into sub-categories), and the judges are expected to be rigorous in making sure that their beers adhere to the guidelines, which are drawn up under the auspices of the Beer Judge Certification Program. The judging takes place over three days, and the judges are split up into small groups. After intense discussions, the judges award gold, silver, and bronze medals for the first, second, and third place beers.

— *Pulped fiction* —
### WATERMELON WARHEAD
Feral Brewing
Perth, Australia
{ feralbrewing.com.au }
BERLINER WEISSE, 2.9%

How to make an award-
winning beer: first of all, get
some watermelons from a
local farm. Then get some
Chardonnay barrels (Feral are
in Swan Valley wine country
in Western Australia). Next,
brew a sour beer (reminiscent
of Berliner Weisse), low in
alcohol. Finally, ferment in the
barrels with lactobacillus, and
then add the pulped watermelons. The result is this masterpiece of a beer that is sweet
as well as sour, quenching and
crisp in its mouthfeel, and so
spritzy in its carbonation that
you might want to keep on
drinking it all day long.

— *Nicely foraged* —
### WU GANG CHOPS THE TREE
Pressure Drop
London, UK
{ pressuredropbrewing.co.uk }
HEFEWEISSE, 3.8%

How about brewing a
Hefeweisse and then adding
foraged herbs? To make things
even more different, let's brew
it at session strength, rather
than the usual 5%. Take a
taste of this creamy, spicy, and
herbal beer and you can see
how Hackney brewery
Pressure Drop turned the
world of wheat beers upside
down when they first brewed
Wu Gang in 2012. Orange-
yellow in color, there are
cloves, bananas, savory herbs,
and a hint of lemon on the
palate, before it finishes with
more pepper and herbs, and a
growing dryness.

— *Remembered lands* —
### THE LOST WORLD OF DOGGERLAND
Poppyland Brewery
Cromer, UK
{ www.poppylandbeer.com }
WHEAT ALE, 4.9%

Before drinking this beer
you should go to Cromer
and stand on the beach and
look out over the North Sea
and try to imagine the large,
low-lying land that once
covered where the water now
is. This was Doggerland, and
brewer Martin Warren, a man
inspired by what was once
there, produced this beer
to celebrate the lost terrain.
This is a wheat beer, which
includes oak-smoked wheat,
sea purslane, sea wormwood,
and fennel seeds — it is gentle
in its acidity, thirst-quenching,
softly smoked, gently
bittersweet, briefly salty, and
dry and fragrant in the finish.

*— The cuddle of caffeine —*

**HOP ARABICA**

Morada Cia Etílica
Curitiba, Brazil

{ moradaciaetilica.com.br }

PALE ALE, 5%

Beer and coffee are the yin and yang of the day, the sun up and sun down — coffee is invariably for the start of the day, beer as the day comes to a close, though naturally both drinks overlap. Maybe it was this sense of polar opposites that Morada Cia Etílica had in mind when it created Hop Arabica — a pale ale flavored with speciality coffee beans grown in the Mantiqueira Mountains of Brazil. The result is a pact between the citrus juiciness of American hops and the acidity and slight caramel notes of the coffee, all of which make for a fascinating drink that takes coffee and beer to a new level.

*— An ooze of yuzu —*

**SAISON DU JAPON**

Kiuchi Brewery
(Hitachino)
Naka, Japan

{ hitachino.cc }

SAISON, 5%

"It's a Saison Jim, but not as we know it," normally farmhouse-lean and flinty. Instead this is a beer with a Saison yeast, alongside the strain of rice usually used to make sake and the juice of the yuzu. The result is a beer with a perfumy, citrus aroma on the nose, a refreshing and gentle breeze of fruitiness. It's juicy, and has a slight acidity in the mid-palate, but there's a sweetness, a bruised fruit fruitiness, a fullness of flavor, and a peppery pungency. The finish has a graininess and a sweetness that hang around. This shows how imaginative Japanese beer can be.

*— Morning in Catalonia —*

**VALLENATO COFFEE PORTER**

Cervesa la Pirata
Súria, Spain

{ cervesalapirata.com }

PORTER, 5.5%

Who made the first coffee beer, and transformed it into an inspiration for the caffeine-fueled chances that brewers have taken in the past few years? (Some might say it was London's Meantime, but others will probably know of an American beer that kicked off the coffee craze.) While we consider the question, let's pour ourselves a glass of this dark chestnut-brown coffee porter and sink into its luscious aromatics of roast coffee beans, cinnamon, licorice, and malt loaf. It's chocolaty, nutty, earthy, coffee-like, and roasty.

— *Grains of the world unite* —
## SURVIVAL STOUT
Hopworks Urban Brewery
Portland, OR, USA
{ hopworksbeer.com }
STOUT, 5.8%

Brewers create beers using malted barley, hops, water, and yeast, and many craft beautiful ornamental drinks out of this simple quartet of ingredients. For Survival, though, brewmaster and Hopworks founder Christian Ettinger thought long and deep about what would go into the mash tun, and used seven different grains: barley, wheat, spelt, quinoa, amaranth, kumat, and oats; cold-brewed coffee was also added. "The idea behind the beer," he says, "was to weave together ancient grains from successful civilizations into a dark and mysterious brew, and then to top it with modern man's survival tool — coffee. Drawing attention to the cereal grains that are seldom used in the modern diet, let alone the brewery, was a fun challenge." Roasted grain and coffee swirl out of the nose, while there's a smooth and creamy mouthfeel, almost mocha-like in its gentleness, and there is also chocolate, hints of vanilla, a nuttiness, more coffee (Java perhaps, or maybe Kenyan), before a pleasing bitterness in the finish. "This beer firmly states that grain, coffee, and beer are all necessary for Survival," says Ettinger. And he's right, you know.

— *Nuts* —

## PEANUT BUTTER MILK STOUT

Tailgate Beer
Nashville, TN, USA
{ tailgatebeer.com }
**MILK STOUT, 5.8%**

You know that dreamy feeling when you put some peanut butter onto a slice of bread? Well, this beer isn't that. It's much more assertive in its peanut crunch, as the dark malts rein in any tendency to peanut butter sweetness, though you still have that lushness, that velvety, nutty smoothness that drew you to peanut butter in the first place. However, here it's allied with a darkness and a slightly charred quality that all seem to work when taken together. There's a dryness in the finish, and a full-bodied presence that has turned a fanciful idea into something that really works.

— *Flower power* —

## ROSÉE D'HIBISCUS

Brasserie Dieu du Ciel!
Saint-Jérôme, Canada
{ dieuduciel.com }
**WHEAT BEER, 5.9%**

Ideas for beers can come from many sources — chance tastings; meetings with brewers; historical archives. This intriguing beer, with its striking hints of pink and delicate floral nose, came about after head brewer Jean-François Gravel had been watching a TV documentary about West African culture. The program showed a woman making Bissap juice, which includes the dried red flowers of *Hibiscus sabdariffa*. This gave Gravel an idea — hibiscus flowers were added to the brewing process, and the result was this fresh and fruity wheat beer that was a hit from the moment it was first served.

— *In the sandpit* —

## LUPONIC DISTORTION

Firestone Walker
Brewing
Paso Robles, CA, USA
{ firestonewalker.com }
**IPA, 5.9%**

Every brewer loves to play, to throw things up in the air. Luponic Distortion is brewmaster Matt Brynildson's chance to muck about in the sandpit — a sandpit full of new, experimental hops. Every three months a different Luponic Distortion allows an emerging hop variety to take its spot in the brewing limelight. First developed in 2016, the debut Luponic was a clean, juicy, and steel-eyed IPA, resonant with piny and tropically fruity notes, and with the kind of finish that suggests a sunny afternoon in a hammock is in order. The power of play indeed.

— *Pre-Reinheitsgebot* —

### ABRAXXXAS

Freigeist Bierkultur
Cologne, Germany
LICHTENHAINER, 6%

Bringing back old beers requires a certain amount of imagination. Ever since they founded Freigeist in 2009, Sebastian Sauer and Peter Esser have had no shortage of imagination as they have resarched forgotten German beers. Here an Alt (what an outrage, a Cologne brewery producing a beer of its neighboring rival!), there an Adambier, and then there is Abraxxxas, a smoky and sour Lichtenhainer that is tart, quenching, smoky-sweet, medium-bodied, and a wonderful evocation of German regional beers before the grip of the Reinheitsgebot put an end to such dreaming.

— *Chocolate calls it* —

### PRALINE

La Sirène Brewing
Melbourne, Australia
{ lasirene.com.au }
STOUT, 6%

Be prepared for an eloquent expression of decadence when drinking this dark and soulful sweet stout. First brewed in 2014, brewery founder Costa Nikias wanted it to express what he sees as the very best of Belgium — chocolate and beer. "We hand-scrape fresh organic vanilla pods (a lot of them) for every brew," he says, "and with toasted cacao nibs and hazelnuts aim to create a praline chocolate experience in a beer." The result is velvety smooth, with vanilla, toasted hazelnuts, and chocolate notes striking poses on the palate, and a stout-like dryness in the finish.

— *Greece catches craft* —

### WEDNESDAY WHEAT IPA (W-DAY)

Septem Microbrewery
Orologio, Greece
{ septem.gr }
IPA, 6%

Today Greece produces a surprisingly large number of excellent beers, but one in particular stands out: an IPA that has a significant amount of wheat in the mix. Not only is Septem brewery making an IPA, but it is also using its imagination and brewing a wheat one (while also using hops from the southern hemisphere). Hazy gold in color, it is fragrant and fruity on the nose alongside hints of banana and clove; the mouthfeel is smooth, which works well with the soft and ripe stone-fruit notes before it finishes bittersweet.

— *Southern comfort* —
## KENTUCKY UNCOMMON
Lervig Aktiebryggeri
Stavanger, Norway
{ lervig.no }
**SOUR BEER, 6%**

— *Exquisite torture* —
## PULLING NAILS
Side Project Brewing
St. Louis, MO, USA
{ sideprojectbrewing.com }
**SOUR BEER, 6%**

— *Nitro niceness* —
## MILK STOUT NITRO
Left Hand Brewing
Longmont, CO, USA
{ lefthandbrewing.com }
**MILK STOUT, 6%**

This is a collaboration between Lervig and To Øl, a cross-border friendship of fermentation influenced by bourbon-making. According to Lervig's brewmaster, Mike Murphy: "Last year I asked To Øl co-founder Tobias Emil Jensen to come up and make a beer with me. He likes our sour beers, and as we had only just begun to play with kettle souring he suggested we make a Kentucky Common recipe based off the classic recipe of using whiskey wash with corn, rye, and barley malt." Southern hemisphere hops were added to give a tropical fruitiness, and the result is a tart, refreshing, juicy beer.

Over at Side Project, who brew their beers at Perennial Artisan Ales, where founder Cory King began his career in beer, Pulling Nails is a continuous experiment in blending different sour and wild beers, and then aging them in a variety of wine barrels for anything up to two years. There is no single Pulling Nails beer: each expression gets its own number with, for instance, #4 being a blend of *bière de Champagne*, wild ale, and the brewery's Saison Pêche Oude Fermier. The results, whatever the number, are fantastically complex beers that demonstrate the art of the blender.

Leave all prejudices of nitro beers at the door when you come to Left Hand's glossy and dreamy Milk Stout Nitro. The original Milk Stout (still available) was brewed "as a lark" according to brewery founder Eric Wallace, and in 2011 this nitro version was first served on draft, and is now one of the brewery's regulars. Soft and creamy in its mouthfeel, the nitro version delivers a rich mocha character alongside chocolate and vanilla with a slight roasty bitterness in the finish. Given the negative connotations of nitro-keg in the past, the creation of this beer was nothing short of inspirational.

— *Chili con cerveza* —
### HOPPY GONZALES
Shenanigans Brewing
Sydney, Australia
{ shenanigansbrewing.com }
**PALE ALE, 6.5%**

Most breweries have their core
range, but many brewers also
like the idea of going off on a
tangent and coming up with
something totally off the wall.
Hoppy Gonzales is this kind of
beer, a kind of let's-see-what-
happens beer, where 42 pounds
(19 kg) of jalapeños have been
added at three different stages
to an American Pale Ale (all
seeded by hand). The result
is a punch of peppery spice
on the nose, while the palate
demonstrates a great balance
between biscuity bittersweetness, citrusy hop character,
and the warmth of the chiles.

— *Smoke and barrels* —
### L'ENFANT TERRIBLE
Brouwerij De Dochter
van de Korenaar
Baarle-Hertog, Belgium
{ dedochtervandekorenaar.be }
**SOUR BEER, 6.5%**

This is a beer that starts life as
one of the brewery's regulars,
Bravoure — a smoked beer
with suggestions of Bamberg's
Rauchbiers in its aromatics
and flavor. Next stage is up to
18 months slumbering in
barrels that once held red
wine. Transformation occurs
as wild yeasts and other
bugs within the wood start to
change the nature of the beer,
making the smokiness more
subtle, and adding tart, gently
sour and woody notes
alongside suggestions of
caramel, ripe dark fruits,
leather, and a pleasing
bittersweetness, all of which
make for a thoughtful beer.

— *Berry intriguing* —
### BALTIC FRONTIER
### SEABUCKTHORN IPA
To Øl
Copenhagen, Denmark
{ to-ol.dk }
**IPA, 6.5%**

Sea buckthorn are little
orange-colored berries found
on the North Sea coast that
normally feed only birds.
To Øl had the idea that they
could also contribute to a
beer. The brewery then added
juniper berries alongside
American hops. The result is
this celebration of a modern
IPA alongside the traditions of
Scandinavian and Baltic brewing. A hazy gold in color, the
nose is citrusy and spicy with
a hint of berries; it's a fruity-
tasting beer with more berries,
some orange and grapefruit,
a thirst-quenching sourness,
and a bittersweet spicy finish.
Intriguing.

— *Wildly different* —
## SHNOODLEPIP
Wild Beer
Shepton Mallet, UK
{ wildbeerco.com }
**SOUR BEER, 6.5%**

Take a couple of guest brewers
and a new brewery whose
aim is to create beers that are
different, and you have
Shnoodlepip. Back in 2013,
Kelly Ryan (formerly of
Thornbridge, now of Fork
Brewing in New Zealand) and
Mark Tranter (founder of Burning Sky) got together with Wild
Beer's brewer Brett Ellis to
produce this eloquent
statement. It's a special
sour, with passion fruit, pink
peppercorns, and hibiscus
flowers, as well as time (four
months) in red wine barrels, and
wild and saison yeast strains.
The result is a tangy, peppery,
funky, fruity, and herbal beer
whose flavor and character
linger long after it is finished.

— *Grape expectations* —
## BIÈRE DE BLANC DU BOIS
Jester King
Austin, TX, USA
{ jesterkingbrewery.com }
**SOUR BEER, 6.7%**

Jester King's founder Jeffrey
Stuffings says: "We love to
blur the lines between wine
and beer. We also love to use
what's around us to make
beer that's unique to a time
and place, and Blanc du Bois
grapes happen to be grown
right down the road from us."
This barrel-aged sour beer
is replete with added grapes,
a golden glow from which
light grape and earthy notes
emerge, with the fruitiness
continuing with the taste
alongside a quenching
tartness and acidity, and a
bone-dry finish.

"THEY WHO DRINK BEER WILL
THINK BEER."
WASHINGTON IRVING, 1819

— *Sherry aid*—
## LITTLE BICHOS MOSCA IPA PX
Mateo & Barnabé
Logroño, Spain
{ mateoybernabe.com }
IPA, 7%

Home for Mateo & Barnabé is an industrial estate on the outskirts of Logroño, provincial capital of La Rioja, Spain. The beers are made and stored in two warehouses, one of which is home to an implacable-looking family of wooden barrels, most of which once held red wine. Now they keep company with a variety of beers, such as IPA PX (released under the umbrella of Little Bichos). This program, according to brewery founder Alberto, "was born from the philosophy of Little Bichos making authentic and experimental beers and giving them a local identity." The brewery managed to get hold of five ancient Pedro Ximenez barrels, and then brewed an IPA featuring seven hops, including Columbus, Centennial, and Simcoe. A long sleep then beckoned. The result is a copper-colored beer with ripe apricot skin on the nose; this fruitiness continues on to the palate, with hints of honeycomb, papaya, orange, and a crisp biscuity finish. This is an elegant and assured beer, but be warned: PX barrels are rare, so if you manage to find this beer, sip it up at once.

— *Finesse in a glass* —
### GALAXY WHITE IPA
Anchorage Brewing
Anchorage, AK, USA
{ anchoragebrewingcompany.com }
IPA, 7%

Brewers' imaginations have
gone into overdrive when it
comes to IPA. Some of these
hybrids are easy to mock (fruit
IPA for instance), but then
we come across Anchorage's
Galaxy White IPA, which uses
the peachy Galaxy hop from the
southern hemisphere, but also
coriander, kumquats, and peppercorns. It is aged in French
oak *foudres* with a Witbier yeast,
before being bottle conditioned
with Brettanomyces and wine
yeast. The result is an exceptionally complex beer of finesse
and elegance, boldly flavored,
light in the body, and sprightly
in the carbonation.

— *Seasonally different* —
### MONT SALÈVE BIÈRE DE NOËL
Mont Salève
Neydens, France
{ labrasseriedumontsaleve.com }
STRONG ALE, 7.2%

What kind of beer would
Father Christmas drink?
Perhaps a glass of Trappist
beer? Or something much
more imaginative? This hazy
gold beer resonates and
pulsates with an end-of-the-
bed stocking fullness of ripe
tropical fruit both on the nose
and on the palate, alongside
a bittersweet hint of fruitcake
and caramel before the bitter
finish. French brewery Mont
Salève has eschewed the
usual spice and sweetness of
Christmas beers, and Santa
Claus might as well.

— *A soothing sipper* —
### ESPRESSO STOUT
Trois Dames
Sainte-Croix,
Switzerland
{ brasserie3dames.ch }
STOUT, 7.2%

This beer is vivid in the glass,
mysterious-looking in its
darkness, luxurious even.
The use of coffee in the brew
(locally roasted beans) is a
clear sign of Trois Dames'
brewing confidence.
Chocolate, freshly brewed
espresso, and a hint of vanilla
swim out of the glass and onto
the nose, while tasting the
beer reveals more rich
chocolate and vanilla before
the espresso character starts
to emerge, and then it's a
journey to a finish with
more chocolate and a roast-
influenced dryness. Trois
Dames' Espresso Stout is a
soothing, smoothing classic.

— *A lush masterpiece* —

## CARIBBEAN CHOCOLATE CAKE
Siren Craft Brew
Wokingham, UK
{ sirencraftbrew.com }
STOUT, 7.4%

Pour this into the glass and marvel at its impenetrable darkness; this is the kind of darkness that could shroud the act of a murderer. On the nose, it's cold coffee, earthy dark chocolate, the kind of raw grown-up chocolate that you didn't find in the chocolate bars you ate as a child. There's also a swirl of creaminess that is reminiscent of condensed milk, of caramel, even — but a caramel tackled to the ground by an interloper with spice on his breath. The beer is creamy and sweet on the palate, juicy, luscious, lubricious, lewd, almost like a milk stout from the wrong side of town. There are also hints of coconut and orange among the luxuriousness on display. Originally brewed in collaboration with Cigar City, it has hand-roasted cacao nibs added to the mix, and is aged on cypress wood: it is surely a master-piece of the imagination.

— *Inspired Weizen* —

## KING HEFFY IMPERIAL HEFEWEIZEN

Howe Sound Brewing

Squamish, Canada

{ howesound.com }

WEIZENBOCK, 7.7%

King Heffy sounds like a cartoon character for kids, maybe even a sinister clown-like figure that hides down alleyways (the label features a glowingly gold but slightly tarnished crown, which might, if you're inclined to dissect such things, suggest failure). On the other hand, all you need to do is see the golden glow of this beer in the glass, and you will be drawn to the ripe banana and cloves aromatics, the brisk carbonation, the ripe fruitiness, and the classic Weizen dry finish to realize that there is nothing to worry about. Mind you, it is 7.7%…

— *Hopless in Ghent* —

## GRUUT BRUIN

Stadsbrouwerij Gruut

Ghent, Belgium

{ gruut.be }

DUBBEL, 8%

Whenever a new brewery or brewpub opens, it is described as "creative," even if it follows the usual path of producing IPA, pale ale, and porter. When Annick De Splenter opened her brewpub Stadsbrouwerij Gruut in 2009, creativity was truly at the hub of her enterprise: the brewery's Gruit beers are based on medieval recipes that use spices such as bog myrtle, wild rosemary, and yarrow (no hops, no IPA). One of her beers is this smooth, chocolaty, and nutty Brune that sits, sleek and glossily chestnut-brown, in the glass beneath a thick head of foam. This is a small piece of brewing history.

— *Vinously vivid* —

## BEERBERA

LoverBeer

Turin, Italy

{ loverbeer.com }

FRUIT BEER, 8%

Adding grape must to beer during fermentation could be seen as crazy, the kind of thing zany breweries do. However, on the other hand, given Italy's reputation as a wine country, it makes sense to marry the juice of the grain with that of the grape. For BeerBera, the amorously named LoverBeer brewery adds freshly pressed Barbera grape juice along with the skins during fermentation before maturing it in oak vats. The result is a complex and refreshingly sour beer with vinous hints on the palate, a sensuous, almost erotic charge — this is a beer to dedicate time to.

— *Boxing clever* —
### CIGAR BOX IPA
Tacoma Brewing
Tacoma, WA, USA
{ tacomabrewing.com }
IPA, 8%

Tacoma Brewing is a Lilliputian brewpub set up by Morgan Alexander in 2012. Their Cigar Box IPA has been aged on Spanish cedar and finished with Brettanomyces yeast. It is complex in its aromatics (cedar, vanilla, sandalwood, and tobacco) and flavor, with a chili-like spiciness on the palate, joined by a deep grapefruit character (please thank the Simcoe hop variety next time you bump into one); there is bracing bitterness and, for those of us who can recall our father's cigar box, a rich, mellow, spicy hint of wood. An altogether fascinating beer.

— *A fizzical collaboration* —
### OUD BEERSEL BZART-LAMBIC
Oud Beersel
Beersel, Belgium
{ oudbeersel.com }
CHAMPAGNE BEER, 8%

Here is a lambic fermented with champagne yeast, a collaboration between classic lambic producer Oud Beersel and Belgian winemaker Domus Ad Fontes. The result is a bottle of elegance. It is earthy and farmhouse-like on the nose, with a grapefruity eloquence in the background; it has a Moussec-like mouthfeel: you could imagine you are drinking a bone-dry champagne. There's more grapefruit on the palate, a soft acidity, and the finish is dry and quenching. Great with a hunk of *formaggio* and slices of Serrano ham.

— *Forest-influenced beer* —
### AMBURANA LAGER
Cervejaria Wäls
Belo Horizonte, Brazil
{ wals.com.br }
DOPPELBOCK, 8.4%

Although Wäls has always looked to the United States for inspiration for its beers, a good measure of its confidence is how it also uses indigenous ingredients. A great example is this strong lager. It spends up to three months maturing on chips of *Amburana* from the Amazon forest (this wood is usually used to age *cachaça*). It is a dark chestnut-colored beer, with notes of woody spice, honey, and vanilla on the nose. The vanilla smoothness continues on the palate, with hints of toast, a light woodiness, and restrained sweetness, courtesy of the malt.

— *Spicing up a Dubbel* —
## SIAMESE TWIN ALE
Uncommon Brewers
Santa Cruz, CA, USA
{ uncommonbrewers.com }
**BELGIAN-STYLE
DUBBEL**, 8.5%

Belgian brewery Uncommon has used Indian coriander, common in the cuisine of the subcontinent, for this beer. As well as this herb, lemongrass and kaffir lime leaves are added, and the result is a complex and comfortable Belgian-style Dubbel, with the uncommon ingredients acting as a counterpoint to the honeyed and caramel notes of the beer. A limey zestiness, a hint of coriander, a quenching tartness, and a bittersweet finish all add to the mellifluous make-up. And all Uncommon beers are organic.

— *The nutty processor* —
## BASTARDA DOPPIA
Birra Amiata
Arcidosso, Italy
{ birra-amiata.it }
**CHESTNUT BEER**, 8.5%

Only one beer style has been developed that can be called truly Italian: chestnut beer. One of the most fêted of the style is this muscular and modestly hopped amber ale from Birrificio Amiata, which, being close to Mount Amiata in Tuscany, where chestnut trees grow in abundance, could not but help make use of the local produce. The result is a rich and inventive beer with honeyed sweetness, and a hint of roast chestnut and dried fruit on the nose. The palate is chocolate, a restrained sweetness, a light toastiness, and more dried fruit leading to a dry finish.

"WHAT CARE I HOW TIME
ADVANCES?
I AM DRINKING ALE TODAY."
EDGAR ALLAN POE, 1848

149

SEVEN MOODS OF CRAFT BEER    IMAGINATIVE

*— Kees-bocking —*
### INDIAN SUMMER DOPPELBOCK
Brouwerij Kees
Middelburg, the Netherlands
{ brouwerijkees.nl }
**DOPPELBOCK, 8.5%**

*— Is it a beer? —*
### CHÂTEAU D'YCHOUFFE
Brasserie d'Achouffe
Achouffe, Belgium
{ achouffe.be }
**BELGIAN STRONG ALE, 9%**

We are not in Munich. We are not in March, when there's a Doppelbock celebration in Munich. We are in the Netherlands instead (and toward the end of the summer, when this beer is released), in the company of one of that country's most inventive and creative brewers, Kees Bubberman. "A bock is sweet, malty, and loads of caramel," he says, "I made mine a little different, using smoked malt and some winter spices such as star anise, cinnamon, and vanilla beans." The result is a chestnut-brown beer that simmers beneath a crema-colored head, while the sweetness of the malt (chocolate and vanilla) vies with hints of smoke and spice to deliver a beer that is at once complex and completely approachable. We are in Kees-land.

Is it a wine? Or a beer? That's the first question you probably ask on sipping this intriguing beer–wine hybrid that has been annually produced since 2013. When I tried the first vintage, I asked the same question as I pondered the ringing, chiming, grape-like notes on the nose, somewhat reminiscent of Sauternes, while digesting the light and delicate fruit (apricot and Muscat orange perhaps) and the restrained sweetness on the palate. It's a fascinating beer, a mixture of one-third grape must (currently from a Burgundy vineyard), and two-thirds wort from Achouffe's golden ale before going onto fermentation. Still pondering, I emailed Chris Bauweraerts, founder of Brasserie d'Achouffe, who replied: "I'd like to describe it as a dessert beer."

— *Bonn goût* —
## IMPERIAL RED ALE
Ale-Mania
Bonn, Germany
{ ale-mania.de }
IMPERIAL RED ALE, 9.2%

In the 2000s, while the rest of the beer-loving world embraced the US craft beer revolution, German brewers seemed happy to continue as they had always done. Not so Fritz Wülfing, who founded Ale-Mania in 2010. Imperial Red Ale was first brewed in 2014 for the World Beer Cup. It didn't win a medal, but Wülfing created a beer that has become one of the company's most popular. Red amber in color, it brims with tropical fruit and caramel sweetness on the nose; on the palate, it's an arc of tropical fruit, pine-like resin, big bitterness, and a caramel sweetness counterpointed with a long, dry finish.

— *Clay time* —
## ETRUSCA
Birra Del Borgo
Borgorose, Italy
{ birradelborgo.it }
SPECIALITY BEER, 9.3%

Italian brewers are noted for their sense of innovation but, in developing Etrusca, Birra del Borgo seem to have gone further than most. They ferment and mature this beer in terracotta amphorae. Originally developed by Borgo's founder, Leonardo Di Vincenzo, with Dogfish Head's Sam Calagione and Le Baladin's Teo Musso, this beer attempts to replicate ancient Etruscan ales with additions of honey, hazelnut flour, and pomegranate. It's an orange-amber-colored beer, with honeyed, herbal, and fruity notes on the nose and palate, and a mineral-like character coming from the clay.

— *The rule of three* —
## DUVEL TRIPEL HOP
Duvel Moortgat
Breendonk-Puurs,
Belgium
{ duvel.com }
BELGIAN GOLDEN ALE,
9.5%

Once a year, Duvel gets a limited release with an extra hop variety added to the usual two that go into this beautiful Belgian beer. For 2016, the brewers selected an experimental hop from the Yakima Valley — HBC 291. The result is a multi-dimensional beer with a juicy, Muscat-like nose, luscious and lubricious, oranges and lemons, sprightly and flighty. It's fruity, with high notes of tangerine, mandarin, and passion fruit, while the dryness in the finish, with its hint of black pepper, could enable you to strike a match on your tongue.

*— Sardinian adventure —*
## BB10
Birrificio Barley
Maracalagonis, Sardinia, Italy
{ barley.it }
**IMPERIAL STOUT, 10%**

Sardinia, home to Birrificio Barley, is an island
with no beer tradition. This gives founder Nicola
Perra a free rein when it comes to imagining
and designing his beers. BB10 is one of them.
Ostensibly it's an Imperial stout, but the
Sardinian influence is the addition of the boiled
must of the local grape variety Cannonau di
Sardegna (or Grenache on the French
mainland). The beer is as dark as Sardinia's
night sky, with a creamy and silky mouthfeel;
there is coffee, caramel, licorice, and chocolate,
as well as intimations of cherry brandy, plus a
vinous hint. It's only made once a year, and it's
well worth hunting down, but until then you'll
just have to imagine it in the glass.

*— Honey, I made a beer —*
## BRACIA
Thornbridge Brewery
Bakewell, UK
{ thornbridgebrewery.co.uk }
**IMPERIAL STOUT, 10%**

This is a beer to wax lyrical about. Soothing,
smoothing, creamy, rustically roasty, burnt, and
burnished, it's a big slab of a beer. It displays
coffee beans, chocolate, almond paste, alcohol,
and fiery bitterness, with a tongue-tingling
bite on the end of the palate; but there is also
sambuca, chocolate-coated coffee beans, and
the bitter bite of chestnut honey, which is the
extra ingredient that the high-spirited brewers
at Thornbridge Brewery add. The chestnut
honey adds an herbal-like sweetness to the
beer, a breakfast honey-coated toast character. This is a reflective beer, and a beer that
demands diligent study.

*— A fall fantasy —*
## AUTUMN MAPLE
The Bruery
Placentia, CA, USA
{ thebruery.com }
**SPECIALITY BEER, 10%**

Every year, come late summer, a growing number of American breweries produce pumpkin beers, a trend that divides beer fans — some think them tasteless, while others regularly fall for the pumpkin-pie spice character. Maybe this divide was in the mind of The Bruery's brewers when they created Autumn Maple, for instead of pumpkin they opted for yam, 440 pounds (200 kg) of which were roasted on a barbeque to be added alongside maple syrup, molasses, and spices. The result is a spicy and fruity amber beer, smooth in the mouthfeel, its alcoholic strength well integrated, and gently bitter in the finish.

*— Bavarian barley wine —*
## X 2.3 BARLEY WINE
CREW Republic Brewery
Munich, Germany
{ crewrepublic.de }
**BARLEY WINE, 10.1%**

This a barley wine. What is so imaginative about that, you might ask, even if it is a bitter and fiery, muscular yet luscious barley wine, peppery, dry and bitter, roasty, toffee-like and tarry, potent and ironclad in its certainty in the glass? For a start, this is a barley wine made in Munich, where strong beers are traditionally Doppelbocks, amber-colored rushes of "liquid bread," originally meant to quell the soul during Lenten fasting. This is a Bavarian barley wine, an imaginative step in a beer society where frowns are still cast at anything outside the norm that has gone before — and for that let us be grateful.

*— Waste not, want not —*
### BEER GEEK BRUNCH WEASEL
Mikkeller (brewed at Lervig)
Copenhagen, Denmark
{ mikkeller.dk }
IMPERIAL STOUT, 10.9%

First of all there was Breakfast Beer Geek, a
sumptuous oatmeal stout to enjoy at brunch
rather than in your pajamas. Then there was
this one, using coffee beans that have passed
through the gut of the civet (a fox-like mammal
from Southeast Asia), and which are then found
and collected from its droppings. Despite what
could be seen as its unsavory source, this is
based on an über-gourmet coffee that makes
for an equally über-gourmet beer: smooth and
soothing, creamy even, it brims with chocolate,
coffee, vanilla, caramel, licorice, and all things
nice. A great example of Mikkeller's imaginative
approach to beer.

*— Hop offensive —*
### UNHUMAN CANNONBALL
Magic Rock Brewing
Huddersfield, UK
{ magicrockbrewing.com }
TRIPLE IPA, 12%

Given that the idea behind the foundation of
Magic Rock in 2011 was to bring the fresh and
fragrant flavors of US West Coast IPAs and pale
ales to the UK, the development of Unhuman
Cannonball comes as no surprise. Brewed once
a year, when American hops are at their
freshest, this is a triple IPA version of the
brewery's standout Cannonball IPA, dry-hopped
in multiple stages to give depth and allow
the hops time to be absorbed. The result is
lemon-gold in color, juicy, bracingly bitter, and
forward-facing in its grapefruit character. If you
want to imagine yourself on the west coast of
America, this is the beer you need.

*— Paraguay meets Delaware —*
## PALO SANTO MARRON
Dogfish Head
Milton, DE, USA
{ dogfish.com }
**AMERICAN BROWN ALE, 12%**

Dogfish Head's founder and brewer Sam Calagione is one of the most imaginative brewers in the United States. For him, brewing is about expanding the boundaries of what we class as beer, and seeing how far his brewers can go. Palo Santo Marron is an American Brown Ale that is aged in massive wooden vats, but these containers are made of *palo santo*, an incredibly hard and aromatic wood from Paraguay that is usually used in wine-making. The result is a beer as dark as the heart of a dense forest, with rich malt, a sweet woodiness, light roastiness, coffee, vanilla, and well-integrated alcohol, all wrapped up with a dry finish.

*— Drink at the world's end —*
## XYAUYÙ
Le Baladin
Piozzo, Italy
{ baladin.it }
**BARLEY WINE, 13.5%**

Jesus turned water into wine, but with Xyauyù, Le Baladin's Teo Musso went one step farther — changing beer into wine. Xyauyù is a moonless-night-dark, strong, and complex barley wine that, after its initial fermentation, is left to mature for between 14 and 18 months before resting in bottle for a while longer. The result is warming and sherry-like, complex and blessed with a restrained but comfortable sweetness: an elegant and esoteric beer that has taken on the character of wine. Musso also ages the beer in a variety of barrels, including rum ones, while the drink-by date on the bottle says it is to be consumed by the end of the world…

— *Sect appeal* —

## DARK LORD IMPERIAL STOUT

Three Floyds Brewing
Munster, IN, USA
{ 3Floyds.com }
IMPERIAL STOUT, 15%

Here is the cult beer of cult beers, available only at the brewery, ticket-only, on one day in April every year: Dark Lord Day. Presumably, it's the Dark Lord who stands on the label, a ferocious warrior with a set of antlers growing out of his helmet, standing in front of a pike-bearing army. Heavy metal thunder. The beer is equally big: brewed with coffee, vanilla, and Indian sugar, and then aged in oak before it is unleashed, a potent and powerful concoction of roasted malt, sweet dried fruit, coffee, vanilla, and chocolate, joined by a viscous, full-bodied mouthfeel and a bittersweet finish. Monstrously imaginative.

— *Beer's outer limits* —

## SAM ADAMS UTOPIAS

Boston Beer
Boston, MA, USA
{ samueladams.com }
VINTAGE BEER, 22–27%

It comes in a mini mash tun, a gleaming copper color. It's thoroughly wicked and potent in its alcoholic strength, up to 23%, depending on the vintage (though one vintage, in the tradition of a fairground high striker, hit 27%). It's also not cheap. However, it's a beer to be sampled, examined, inhaled, shared with good friends, and tasted, rather than gulped and argued over. Some think its sweetness a poison, others adore its complexity and end-of-the-night classicism; this is beer taken to the limit, held over a cliff edge, taken backward and forward, merged with maple syrup, aged in a variety of barrels, and looked after as if it was an Old Master. Drink it once and you won't forget it.

*— A battleship of a beer —*

# SINK THE BISMARCK!

BrewDog
Ellon, UK
{ brewdog.com }
IMPERIAL IPA (AND SOME), 41%

I was once at BrewDog's brewery and, during
the tour of the brewing floor (the rattle of
bottles and cans, hoses snaking across the
surface, earnest men and women checking this
and that), co-founder James Watt stood outside
a container and invited me in: "This is where we
leave Sink the Bismarck!" he said. A wreath of
cold air escaped like a ghost, and I declined
the invitation. When it was released, this
formidable beer claimed to be the strongest of
its kind in the world (until a German brewery
turned up as a usurper), although many asked
how could something so strong be classed as a
beer (and an IPA at that). Perhaps this is where
the container is symbolic — to get a beer this
strong, a process called fractional freezing is
used, where the beer is frozen and the alcoholic
strength becomes more concentrated. It
doesn't really sound orthodox, but, on the other
hand, Sink the Bismarck! is whiskey-like in its
sweetness and strength, bringing forth vanilla,
boozy heat, caramel, a sway of citrus, and an
oily mouthfeel that make it a beer to be tried
at least once.

PREP THE KITCHEN, LAY THE TABLE,
AND POUR ONE OF THESE BEERS, ALL
OF WHICH IN ONE WAY OR ANOTHER
HAVE A PLACE ALONGSIDE A DISH,
WHETHER IT'S SOMETHING SIMPLE
OR A CHALLENGE THAT WOULD HAVE
JAMIE OLIVER SCRABBLING FOR
SUPERLATIVES.

**GASTRONOMIC**

# BEER & FOOD MATCHING

**B**eer has always been served with food, although commonly it was Guinness with a plate of oysters or the landlord's steak and ale pie. There have been brave attempts to plow various furrows, as with 1955's *Beer and Vittles* by noted food writer Elizabeth Craig. Her husband, war correspondent and journalist Arthur Mann, supplied a few paragraphs in the introduction, part of which recalled an old tradition of adding spice to beer and then mulling it: "And I recall one cold and depressing night during the last war when I went to the cellar, fetched up my last pint of extra-strong ale, poured it into a pewter mug, added a pinch of ground cinnamon, plunged a red-hot poker into the liquid and finished up with as fine a mulled drink as man could ask for. As preparation for sleeping through an air-raid I discovered nothing to equal it."

This all sounds very exciting, but flicking through the book we come on a mish-mash of postwar British cuisine's emphasis on boiling stuff, roasting, adding gravy, creating cheese straws, or offering up an ale and mint cup (which also features Chablis) — there is even the seductive siren call of stewed cabbage.

1972 then saw Carole Fahy's *Cooking With Beer*, which was dedicated "To John, who likes his pint." Presumably this was her husband, since the blurb at the back of the book states she is married (and lives in Weybridge). The accompanying photo showed her smiling at the camera, over a mixing dish filled with perhaps cake material, spatula in one hand and a brown bottle of something in the other.

"When I started this book I was amazed at the number of my friends who had never heard of cooking with beer," she wrote in the introduction. I wonder what her friends thought about such dishes as beer ratatouille, chicken Flemish-style (light ale is the beer constituent) and — a particular nightmare of mine — tripe in ale.

As the decades passed and the beer revolution girdled the world, the idea of beer and food matching has grown and grown, especially in the United States with champions such as Garrett Oliver, Lisa Morrison, Lucy Saunders, and John Holl, who have all written on the subject, influencing breweries and suggesting matches. Beer dinners are commonplace wherever good beer is drunk.

But what is beer and food matching about? Is it about the occasion, when beer intensifies

the flavor of the food, and adds something to it? Or alternatively is it about when the ingredients in the dish lift the beer skyward and reveal a hitherto unknown dimension? Or could it be when the two of them collide and come up with something totally new — a gastronomic particle accelerator?

Harmony is important: it's akin to the moment when the woodwind, the strings, and the brass all come together in one grand symphonic hug, perhaps during Schubert's Ninth Symphony or a great shambling moment in Elgar's transcription of the Bach Fantasia & Fugue in C Minor when all seems lost, when all seems chaos, but as the instruments all seemingly topple over, order asserts itself and harmony returns.

For me it's about bringing flavors together and then letting them get on with each other — although it doesn't always happen when matching beer and food. There are some combinations that do not work, and which create a dissonant experience on the palate. I made *moules marinières* once with an English pale ale and the long boil gave a harsh, bitter note to the broth thanks to the concentration of hops; cheese — artisanal Cheshire — as I found out once, with a Czech Pilsner does not work. With each swig of the beer, the dairy fats seem to separate and become oleaginous.

It is not rocket science, it's not the black arts — it's trial and experiment, it's getting things wrong only so that you can get them right the next time. It's the better moments of punk rock or heavy metal thunder, your favorite jeans, frayed and frowning at the damage that time has done, a revelation that wine does not have all the best tunes. It's beer and food.

Times have so changed now when we consider beer's role with food. One of the most enjoyable aspects of beer at the moment is that — beyond the geeky paroles and parades of nomenclature with beers made with baguettes or more hops than is decent — there is a real interest in what beer can bring to the table, what the flavor profiles are, how it can co-exist with or even subsistute for wine. It's been a long march and it's still continuing.

Federico Fellini once remarked: "There is no end. There is no beginning. There is only the infinite passion of life." The Italian director of *La Dolce Vita*, *8½*, and *Amarcord* was presumably a wine-drinker, so he probably didn't have beer and food matching in mind when he made this remark, if he hadn't he should have.

— *Seafood success* —

## TARAS BOULBA
Brasserie de la Senne
Brussels, Belgium
{ brasseriedelasenne.be }
BELGIAN BLONDE, 4.5%

An appetizing bitterness runs through the DNA of de la Senne's beers, which makes them stand out from those of many other Belgian brewers who use spices and candy sugar in their recipes, and shy away from using too many hops. "We hate spices," the brewery's co-founder, Yvan De Baets, once told me. "I have nothing against their use, but it is easy to use them to mask brewing deficiencies." Taras Boulba is one of the brewery's bestsellers, bright and golden, quenching and citrusy, crisp and brisk in its carbonation, and bitter and dry in the finish. For a beer so low in alcohol it has a lot of heft, which means it's ideal with grilled Gulf shrimp.

— *Put the stew on* —

## TELENN DU
Brasserie Lancelot
Roc-Saint-André, France
{ brasserie-lancelot.com }
SPECIALITY BEER, 4.5%

Brittany has long had a thriving beer culture, with Brasserie Lancelot being one of its leading lights. Founded in 1990, its first beer was the herb-flavored Cervoise Lancelot. Several years later, Telenn Du appeared, a so-called *Bière de Blé Noir*, or black wheat beer, which is made with Breton-grown buckwheat (despite its name, buckwheat is not a wheat but related to sorrel and rhubarb). The result is a pitch-black beer with roasted grain and licorice pulsating on the nose, while the mouthfeel and flavor have licorice, dark fruit, and a whisper of chocolate and coffee, before its dry and bittersweet finish. Gastronomically speaking, a Breton *pot-au-feu* is an amiable companion.

**WEIZEN**
Bierland
Blumenau, Brazil
{ bierland.com.br }
WEISSBIER, 4.7%

Imagine you are in the center of Munich and fancy a classic Bavarian breakfast of Weisswurst sausage, pretzels, and a glass of Weissbier. Then let's change continents. If you go to Bierland's hometown of Blumenau in Brazil (founded by German immigrants in the 19th century), this is exactly what you can experience. The town has remained resolutely Germanic in its beery identity, with its Oktoberfest the second largest in the world.

This Weissbier is orange-yellow, with a fluffy cute head of snow-white foam. There's an effervescent, slightly fruity and lightly spicy character before its refreshing finish.

— *Cheese's best friend* —
**HEFEWEIZEN**
Occidental Brewing
Portland, OR, USA
{ occidentalbrewing.com }
WEISSBIER, 4.5%

Portland is the home of ultra-hoppy beers. Occidental go against the grain and opt for German styles as their modus operandi. As well as this Hefeweizen, they produce Kölsch, Altbier, Dunkel, and Pilsner (Czech-style, just to be even more different). You have to be confident of your brewing skills to take on the old world, and Hefeweizen is a great example of the brewery's skills. It's crammed with banana and cloves on the nose and palate, and has a crisp and brisk carbonation that is both refreshing and ideal with goat's cheese or a creamy Camembert.

163

GASTRONOMIC

SEVEN MOODS OF CRAFT BEER

"A MEAL OF BREAD, CHEESE AND
BEER CONSTITUTES THE PERFECT
FOOD."
QUEEN ELIZABETH I OF ENGLAND,
16TH CENTURY

— *Meat smoke beer* —
## GHISA
Birrificio Lambrate
Milan, Italy
{ birrificiolambrate.com }
STOUT, 5%

Birrificio Lambrate is a pioneer of modern artisanal brewing in Milan, having first brewed its beers in 1996 at the back of its own pub, which it still owns. As was common with many new Italian breweries, it was not afraid of beer and food matching, and you can also match its peerless beers at the Lambrate restaurant, which opened in 2011. Ghisa is the brewery's smoked stout, which is made with birch-smoked Bavarian malt added to the mix. It's not a Rauchbier, but something less assertively smoky, while its stout background gives a hint of creaminess in the mouthfeel, as well as coffee and chocolate notes on the nose and the palate. The finish is delicately bitter and dry, but there's also a richness and a hint of saltiness in the background, which makes it an enviable companion to something like grilled mackerel. And in the interests of gastronomic experimentation, trying it with a plate of the best Italian charcuterie (*prosciutto* and *coppa*) will yield some gustatory surprises.

*— The griller —*
### RAUCHBIER
Cervejaria Bamberg
São Paulo, Brazil
{ cervejariabamberg.com.br }
SMOKED BEER, 5.2%

*— Flower power —*
### FLORA RUSTICA
Upright
Portland, OR, USA
{ uprightbrewing.com }
SAISON, 5.2%

*— Porter and pretzel —*
### BLACK BUTTE PORTER
Deschutes Brewery
Bend, OR, USA
{ deschutesbrewery.com }
PORTER, 5.2%

The idea of smoked beer might sound a little odd. But then maybe you've never rhapsodized in the company of friends before a campfire; or even enjoyed the fieriness of lapsang souchong tea. Cervejaria Bamberg showed no such concerns when they set themselves up to the west of São Paulo in 2005 and went on to name themselves after the city where smoked beer rules. Their version of a Franconian classic is smoky, dry, caramel-sweet, medium-bodied, and even has a hint of the campfire, around which you might want to set yourself up grilliing some sausages.

On a sunny day lunch is best served with a green salad with juicy tomatoes. And to drink? Let us pour a glass of pale yellow Portland-derived Saison, crowned with its egg-white head of foam. It's a Saison, though with added yarrow and calendula, alongside the US hops and jazzy Belgian-style yeast, which makes for an herbal, spicy (some coriander seed and black pepper perhaps), citrus, briskly carbonated beer that almost acts as an extra dressing for the salad that makes us feel so good.

It's creamy and chocolaty, there's mocha sweetness balanced by roastiness; it's an engaging mouthful, an easy-drinking dark beer, so why bother considering it with food? One reason. When I visited the brewery's tap and restaurant in Portland, I stood at the bar and ordered a pint and then asked for chicken liver mousse and a honey-mustard pretzel. The creaminess of the beer and pâté linked arms, and the saltiness and crunch of the pretzel contrasted perfectly with the sweetness of the beer.

166

*— Alt-Xmas matching —*
**WINTER ALE**
Oppigårds Bryggeri
Hedemora, Sweden
{ oppigards.com }
STRONG ALE, 5.3%

It's Christmas Day in the UK. Turkey, as usual, is on the table. Pour yourself a glass of Oppigårds Winter Ale and dare to change the plan, start to drink and think differently. This Swedish ale is roasty, chocolaty, and mocha-like, and then there's citrus, dried fruits, a grainy huskiness, a malty sweetness that doesn't over-extend itself; there's a sleekness about its chestnut-brown color and tight white head. What do you want to eat? Dump the turkey, and pick up some pickled herring, in which the sour-sweetness of the fish envelops itself in the dark bittersweetness of the beer to create Christmas harmony.

*— Tex-Mex to go —*
**SOVINA IPA**
Cerveja Sovina
Porto, Portugal
{ sovina.pt }
IPA, 5.4%

Start with a Texan-style taco, deep-fried, filled with flakes of white fish, spicy salsa, a sprinkling of the heat of jalapeño, and the cooling of yogurt or sour cream. Now choose something to drink, something that will stand up to the heat, something that will refresh the mouth, cleanse the palate, and lift the sweetened blandness of the fish higher. Try Sovina IPA, with its frisky carbonation for starters, a full-bodied bittersweet and fruity IPA with a pungent, sticky, resiny nose, and a mid-palate erotically charged citrusiness, all leading to a dry finish.

*— Hi Stilton! —*
## AMARILLO SOUR
Chorlton Brewing Company
Manchester, UK
{ chorltonbrewingcompany.com }
SOUR BEER, 5.4%

Slowly and quietly, Chorlton continues a journey from Manchester's suburbs that somehow incorporates the palate-puckering personality of sour beer (sometimes with added Brettanomyces) with the extra dimension of perfectly picked hop character. There is also a utilitarianism about the way they present themselves to the world: plain cans, not much noise on social media, a slow deliberation about the beers they make — and yet, what wonderful beers. This cunning little number is hazy when poured and dark orange in color; it's gently acidic in the background of the nose, with a suggestion of bruised grapefruit, or maybe flavored balsamic vinegar. On the palate, it's juicy and tart, an overflow of juiciness, grapefruit pushing a cart along with all its earthly belongings. An expressive, assertive, takes-no-nonsense grapefruit, with saltiness in the background and a dryness and a late emergence of a white grape-like fruitiness, while the finish is tart and tantalizing. It's a friendly beer, so friendly that as soon as a sweaty, pungent, salty Stilton passes by it's got its arm 'round the shoulder, friendly and inviting it to join in the journey.

"A CZECH NEVER SAYS THAT HE'S GOING OUT TO HAVE 'A FEW BEERS,' AND HE NEVER COUNTS THE BEERS WHILE HE'S HAVING THEM. YOU GO OUT FOR A BEER."
TIMOTHY O. HALL, 2005

— *Seafood serenade* —
## SOUR GRAPES
Lovibonds
Henley-on-Thames,
UK
{ www.lovibonds.com }
SOUR BEER, 5.4%

Sour Grapes, one of the first English sours, was described as a mistake of fermentation (it's barrel-aged in French Pinot Noir barrels). It's made for plates of seafood (as well as for salted almonds, slices of chorizo, and olives): the muscular grapefruit fruitiness, sharp tartness, mid-palate juiciness, and citrus-edged finish add something to a plate of North Sea shrimps, drawing out the salty sweetness, and adding an extra level of flavor to both shrimp and beer. It's gastronomic and contemplative in equal measure.

— *Through a dish darkly* —
## DARK LAGER
Klášterní Pivovar
Strahov
Prague, Czech Republic
{ klasterni-pivovar.cz }
DARK LAGER, 5.5%

You're in Prague at Klášterní Pivovar Strahov, which brews its own beer. First order the food: pork hock, its skin glistening, roasted in dark beer, with mustard, apple sauce, and horseradish, alongside dumplings. Then order a glass of the brewpub's Dark Lager, a bittersweet, chocolaty, dry, and roasty beer with great depth in its flavor, a beer that as well as being the lifeblood of the dish's sauce is also an incredible compliment. It lifts the flavors, its carbonation cuts through the fattiness of the meat, and also scrubs the palate clean after each mouthful.

— *The muscular one* —
## MA MÈRE SPÉCIALE
De Leite
Ruddervoorde, Belgium
{ www.deleite.be }
SPÉCIALE BELGE, 6%

Mussels and frites is one of the great gustatory table-toppers of Belgium, a dish of sweet juicy seafood, married with crisp, salty fried potato. Beer is a natural partner (often the beer ends up in the pan as well), as this Spéciale Belge, from a small brewery in western Flanders, so aptly and joyfully demonstrates. Amber-gold in the glass, it has pear drops and a fruity sweetness on the nose, followed by a lemony citrus fruitiness, a dry grain malt character, and a clean bitter finish. When sipped with mussels and chips, it's a clear example of beer and food harmony.

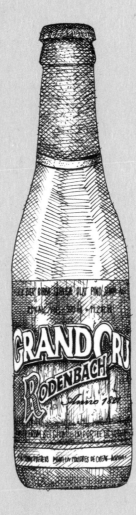

— *Best with venison* —

## GRAND CRU
Rodenbach
Roeselare, Belgium
{ palm.be/en/rodenbach }
FLEMISH RED, 6%

Rodenbach is one of the great survivors of the beer world, having been founded in 1821. It is famous for its unique and world-acclaimed Flemish Red beers, which are a blend of old and young beer, with the old having spent up to two years in massive oak tuns or *foeders*. These *foeders*, of which there are 294, are housed in a special building that could be called the Cathedral of Sour Beers, a silent space of several floors where the beers sleep the sleep of the just, while wild yeasts within the wood work away and produce lactic acid and lower the pH of the beer until the brewing team adjudges them to be ready for blending. Grand Cru, as the name might suggest, is the imperious member of the family, a mixture of one-third young beer and two-thirds beer that has been matured for two years in the *foeders*. On the palate there are an acidity and a fruitiness that match each other, followed by a woody character, vinousness, acidity, and an undercurrent of sweetness. This beer is elegant and assured of itself, and has a great depth of flavor and a soft acidity that makes it an ideal match for a venison casserole.

— *The desserter* —
**AFTERLIGHT**
The Rare Barrel
Berkeley, CA, USA
{ therarebarrel.com }
SOUR BEER, 6%

If the beers of Rare Barrel were refracted through a prism, it would be the red ales, gueuzes, and lambics of Belgium that would emerge. Based in California, the first stage of Rare Barrel's beer is done elsewhere (the boil and the hopping) and then fermentation and conditioning continue in barrels, of which they have more than 800. Afterlight is a dark sour, aged in fresh wine barrels, with rich chocolate and cherry notes joined by layers of vanilla from the oak. A slice of cheesecake and you're set.

— *Currying favor* —
**FEMME FATALE BRETT**
Evil Twin Brewing
Copenhagen, Denmark
{ eviltwin.dk }
IPA, 6%

This is a Belgian-style IPA fermented 100% with Brettanomyces — a bold move. Evil Twin are Danish, but they're also gypsy brewers and this beer was made at Westbrook in the USA. In the glass, it's orange-copper in color, and you can immediately smell the earthy, horse-blanket notes on the nose, cellar-like almost with a citrus brightness in the background. There's fruit, peppery spiciness, tartness and tanginess, bitterness and acidity on the palate, all of which suggest it would be ideal with a Thai red curry.

— *Get the barbie on*—
**IHL**
Camden Town Brewery
London, UK
{ camdentownbrewery.com }
STRONG LAGER, 6.2%

Here lager meets IPA to create India Hells Lager, or IHL, and the two of them get on famously in the glass. This incredibly drinkable mash-up of the two beer styles was launched by Camden in 2014 and immediately acclaimed for its delicate fruitiness (think a sweet, sun-stroked bowl of tropical fruit), smooth mouthfeel, and Sahara-like dry finish. It's refreshing and zesty on the palate, and resonant in its bitter and dry finish. It's exceptional with a BBQ, but can also easily make friends with a salty, pungent blue cheese.

— *Beer and food greatness* —

## ORVAL

Brasserie d'Orval
Villers-devant-Orval,
Belgium
{ orval.be }
**BELGIAN ALE, 6.2%**

In an empty restaurant in the Wallonian town of Tournai, I asked for a beer. A young waiter offered me Chimay Bleu, Stella Artois, Leffe, and the classic Trappist beer Orval. I pointed at the last named, and was served a beautiful-looking glass of Orval, sparkling gold in color with a snow-white head of foam. Then the food came: turbot in a shrimp sauce, with which the Orval faultlessly slipped into line. The dish brought out the creamy texture and citrusy notes of the beer, while the beer's brisk carbonation cut through the cream of the sauce.

— *The versatile one* —

## DR. CALIGARI

Birrificio Toccalmatto
Fidenza, Italy
{ birratoccalmatto.com }
**BERLINER WEISSE,
6.3%**

Parma means two things: cheese and ham. However, after Bruno Carilli launched Toccalmatto just outside the city in 2008, beer is now also on the menu. Dr. Caligari is a Berliner Weisse, which has had plenty of fresh raspberries added during conditioning. The result is a dry and tart beer, a sparky, perky beer that has lemons and raspberries on the nose, followed by a soft mouthfeel, a quenching tartness, and a berry-influenced juiciness. Perfect with a creamy blue cheese, homemade ice cream, or grilled scallops.

— *The rib-tickler* —

## SHAPE SHIFTER

Fourpure Brewing
London, UK
{ fourpure.com }
**IPA, 6.4%**

This is a US West Coast IPA cooked up in a railway arch in Bermondsey, and just one sniff of its glorious tropical fruit-and-chive-like aromatics is enough to transport you to the Pacific coast. It's earthy, sticky, resiny, bold, and boisterous, almost as if an orange has donned a leather jacket and hop cones are swaggering along like Brando in *The Wild One*. It's a big beer, bittersweet and citrusy on the palate with pine notes (a forest after rain); there's also a warm juiciness about its mouthfeel, with all these elements suggesting that it would be a fantastic companion to a rack of spicy, saucy ribs.

— *Fish, chips, and beer*—
### SUPER KROON
Brouwerij de Kroon
Neerijse, Belgium
{ brouwerijdekroon.be }
PALE ALE, 6.5%

There's a conundrum about pale ale. For a start, when we get a glass of pale ale, it's not pale but, like Kroon's Super, it's usually amber, although other pale ales can be copper, golden, or even chestnut, so the name of the beer style is not always to do with the color. On the other hand, judging the beer as a beer, here we find a brisk carbonation, a flurry of citrus orange notes on the palate alongside a slight toffee-like sweetness, and the kind of assertive dry finish on which you could strike a match. Without question, the perfect beer for fish and chips.

— *The charcuterie pleaser* —
### LA ROUSSE
Brasserie du Mont Blanc
La Motte-Servolex, France
{ brasserie-montblanc.com }
BIÈRE DE GARDE, 6.5%

There's an intriguing tale about the water used in all the beers produced by Mont Blanc: it comes from a catchment area beneath the eponymous mountain and is trucked in regularly. It obviously does the trick, since the brewery keeps on winning awards. La Rousse is the brewery's roguish *bière de garde*, an amber-colored beer topped with a tempting head of foam. It is smooth and polished on the palate, with a caramel sweetness on the nose followed by a slight bitterness and dryness in the finish. If you have a plate of charcuterie alongside some pickled gherkins, then this is the beer that would tumble and tantalize the dish.

— *Time for Pad Thai* —
### LEON
Omnipollo
Stockholm, Sweden
{ omnipollo.com }
PALE ALE, 6.5%

A Belgian-style pale ale,
but with a difference: this
time, the gypsy brewers
of Omnipollo have let a
champagne yeast loose during
fermentation, which gives
a brisk carbonation and a
Moussec-like mouthfeel. This
is hazy gold in color sitting
beneath a billowing white
head. There are peach and
tropical fruit notes whizzing
about on the nose, more fruit
and hints of herbal notes and
spice on the palate, and a dry
finish. It's the carbonation
that does the work when it
comes to gastronomy, though,
scrubbing the palate clean
between each mouthful of
Pad Thai.

— *Pizza action* —
### TLUSTÝ NETOPÝR
### (FAT BAT)
Pivovar Antoš
Slaný, Czech Republic
{ pivovarantos.cz }
IPA, 6.7%

The American satirist Dave
Barry once said: "Without
question, the greatest
invention in the history of
mankind is beer. Oh, I grant
you that the wheel was also
a fine invention, but the
wheel does not go nearly as
well with pizza." And pizza
(Neapolitan please) is just
the right dish to accompany
this Czech rye IPA with its
full-on bitterness (especially
in the finish), plus hints of rye,
citrus, and tropical fruit, and
a full-bodied mouthfeel. Pizza
is an easygoing dish, with
Tlustý Netopýr being equally
easygoing, which makes for a
perfect match.

— *Morocc'n'roll* —
### WEIZENBOCK
Pivovar Matuška
Broumy, Czech
Republic
{ pivovarmatuska.cz }
WEIZENBOCK, 6.8%

Imagine you are eating
a fruity lamb tagine: rich,
spicy, and meaty. Now you
need a beer. Off you go to the
Czech Republic to Pivovar
Matuška and its intensely
malty Weizenbock (a beer
style that makes a detour
to Bavaria). Amber in color,
there's a classic Weizen
clove-and-banana note on
the nose, but it's when the
beer laps around the mouth
that it really starts to show off:
honey, malty sweetness, stone
fruit fruitiness, more banana,
high carbonation, and a clasp
of citrusiness. It's full-bodied
and fabulously favorable to a
Moroccan tagine.

*— Brownie points —*
## PADRINO CHOCOLATE VANILLA
### Edge Brewing
### Barcelona, Spain
{ edgebrewing.com }
**PORTER, 6.9%**

If we think of a beer that would accompany a chocolate brownie with the faithfulness of a carriage dog, that would be a comfortable you-can-tell-me-everything friend, we might be thinking of this fudge-like, vanilla-rich, citrusy-fruity porter from Barcelona, from a brewery that is a great example of the growing Catalonian thirst for beers (Madagascan vanilla beans and cocoa nibs are added to the brewery's porter for this hit of luxury). Chocolate brownie, meet Padrino Chocolate Vanilla — I think the two of you will get on very well.

*— Raspberry fool —*
## CHOCARRUBICA
### Birrificio Grado Plato
### Chieri, Italy
{ gradoplato.it }
**STOUT, 7%**

Chocarrubica emerged after the brewery's founder, Sergio Ormea, watched a TV documentary which showed American GIs handing out chocolate bars to Sicilian kids in World War II. The idea of merging carobs and chocolate shone, and Chocarrubica was born. Mahogany in color, the beer has a lustrous, chocolaty nose, with hints of hop dankness. It's vinous and chocolaty in the mouth, busily bitter on the finish; there's also a cherry-like sweetness in the mid-palate. There's a smooth and creamy oiliness in the mouth. A glass with a bowl of freshly picked raspberries would be divine.

*— Stout Thai-in —*
## EXPORT STOUT
### Boundary
### Belfast, UK
{ boundarybrewing.coop }
**STOUT, 7%**

Northern Ireland is experiencing a great wave of small breweries intent on producing beers with flavor and character. Most impressive is Boundary. Their Export Stout is a soothing, collectively cool, flippantly fruity, and graciously elegant beer with chocolate liqueur hints, ripe dark plums, booze-soaked Californian raisins, and mocha coffee on the nose, while the palate is fruity, creamy, chocolaty, initially light and nimble before its alcoholic weight takes over. A bowl of Thai green curry, with its spice, coconut creaminess, and texture of the chicken would act as exemplary company to this beer.

— *Sweet-talkin'* —

### CARAMELIZED CHOCOLATE CHURRO BALTIC PORTER

Moody Tongue
Chicago, IL, USA
{ moodytongue.com }
BALTIC PORTER, 7%

The name tells it all: this is a decadent beer that is a dead cert for squiring creamy, sweetish desserts such as crème caramel, or even chocolate bread pudding. No chocolate or churros were harmed in its making, but you wouldn't know that, such is the preponderance of vanilla, chocolate, and caramel notes on the nose and palate, which are stopped from being too sweet by a clean finish. Given that Moody Tongue's brewmaster, Jared Rouben, has a previous life as a top-class chef, you would expect nothing less.

— *Slow food and slow beer* —

### MODUS OPERANDI

Wild Beer
Shepton Mallet, UK
{ wildbeerco.com }
WOOD-AGED OLD ALE,
7%

Anglo-Belgian-US brewing influences flitter like bats in the night when it comes to explaining the approach of this brewery in rural Somerset. Among the beers produced are a Saison with Brettanomyces yeast, a West Country lambic, and this oak-aged old ale. This was their debut beer, and remains exemplary. Originally brewed as an old ale and then aged in bourbon barrels, it is a lush and generous beer with a stunningly complex nose that ranges from earthy to milk chocolate to vinous to cherry and balsamic vinegar. On the palate, there's a wild chocolate note accompanied by an earthiness, chocolate, cherry, and soft vanilla, and a generous bitter finish. Anyone for Somerset beef carbonnade?

GASTRONOMIC

SEVEN MOODS OF CRAFT BEER

"BECAUSE BEER IS FOOD: IN COOKING, AT THE TABLE, AND BY THE GLASS..."
LUCY SAUNDERS

*— Open the oysters —*
### GYPSY PORTER
Pivovar Kocour
Varnsdorf, Czech
Republic
{ www.pivovar-kocour.cz }
**BALTIC PORTER, 7.2%**

I was at the Slunce ve Skle
beer festival in Plzeň in 2012
when the best beer of the
festival was announced.
Next to me was Max, an
Argentine beer blogger, who
had designed this beer with
Pivovar Kocour and an English
brewery. Max's beer won. We
carried on drinking this dark
Baltic porter with its fantasia
of flavors that included coffee,
licorice, roastiness, and a
tropical fruitiness (thanks
to the use of Citra) — and
then I had a revelation. This
would be ideal for oysters,
the sweetness gelling with
the saltiness. Not long after
I got the chance to try the
combination — it worked.

*— Coffee and cake —*
### C.R.E.A.M.
Sixpoint
Brooklyn, New York
City, NY, USA
{ sixpoint.com }
**CREAM ALE, 7.2%**

It's late morning, and instead
of another coffee how about
delving into this cream ale?
It's a blond-colored beer, with
golden highlights and a thin
creamy head of foam. Cream
ales are very much a minority
taste, veering toward light
maltiness, refreshing rather
than complex. However, by
blending in cold-brewed
coffee, Sixpoint had come up
with a beer that could just as
easily replace your morning
mocha, and don't forget to
have a slice of homemade
coffee cake on hand, as the
crisp and brisk carbonation
will cut through the cake's
sweetness with every
mouthful.

*— Time for tacos —*
### BEER GEEK BREAKFAST
Mikkeller
Copenhagen, Denmark
{ mikkeller.dk }
**OATMEAL STOUT, 7.5%**

Sometimes it's a good idea to
have something rather simple
to accompany your beer. Even
though its name suggests
something in the morning,
Beer Geek Breakfast is the
kind of beer you can drink at
any time of the day—although,
given that it has coffee in the
brew, maybe you shouldn't
have it too late. It's the beer
that kicked off Mikkeller's
gypsy brewing career, a
creamy and smooth, pitch-
black, oatmeal stout with
chocolate, coffee, smoke, and
dark fruits all over the place.
It's sleek and elegant, and
might just be ideal with pulled
beef brisket tacos.

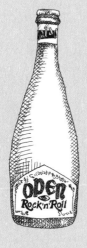

*— The seafood sipper —*
## OPEN ROCK'N'ROLL
Le Baladin
Piozzo, Italy
{ baladin.it }
PALE ALE, 7.5%

Let's have some freshly cooked, deep-fried,
crunchy calamari with a handful of prawns,
the lemon juice squeezed on the paper plate
teasing out a fragrance. This is exactly what I
had at a small market in Bologna on a Sunday
evening when the city was starting to wind
down. Along from the seafood stand, there
was a small Birra Baladin bar from which
I got a large glass of Open Rock'n'Roll, an
American-style pale ale, bright and vivid, with
citrusy notes on nose and palate, alongside an
undercurrent of black pepper. The citrusiness,
crispness, spiciness, and dry finish thoroughly
engaged with the seafood and, so fascinated
was I with the match, that I went back for more
as Sunday faded away.

*— The hotpot hero —*
## HOUTGERIJPTE ROOK DUBBELBOCK
Speciaalbierbrouwerij
Duits & Lauret
Everdingen, the Netherlands
{ duitslauret.com }
DOPPELBOCK, 7.5%

It's a Doppelbock, but not how a German
brewmaster would create it. For their riff on this
most wintery and intense of beer styles, Duits
& Lauret add up to 40% of smoked malt to the
grist, which unsurprisingly gives the beer a light
and elegant element of smokiness on both the
nose and palate (think an autumnal bonfire a
couple of fields away). When you taste this
dark, dark brown beer you will also get hints
of caramel, raisins, a creaminess on the
mouthfeel, and a light roastiness, all wrapped
up in an intensity of flavor. It's a cold night and
the beer is strong, so make yourself a beef stew
(Flemish-style perhaps), and enjoy the way the
beer and the dish cohabit.

— *The spice cutter* —
### JAI ALAI
Cigar City Brewing
Tampa, FL, USA
{ cigarcitybrewing.com }
IPA, 7.5%

You feel like some spice
on your plate, maybe an
enchilada filled with ground
beef, sliced tomatoes,
chopped chiles, a good dose
of fajita, and grated cheese.
Now, how about a beer that
will stand up to the heat,
cut through the spice, and
lift the bright assemblage of
flavors and generally make
life worthwhile? How about
Jai Alai, a big brute of an IPA,
bursting with tropical fruit,
citrus, and pine on the nose,
which serves as an entrée to
the main course of more fruit,
pine, a light malt sweetness,
and a long finish bristling with
bitterness and dryness?

— *The vegetarian option* —
### GREAT RETURN
Hardywood Park Craft
Brewery, Richmond,
VA, USA
{ hardywood.com }
IPA, 7.5%

Beer matched with vegetarian
food? Why not? I was once in
a small restaurant in South
London on a hot summer's
night with a plate of *girolles*,
sweet corn, orange, and
allspice butter in front of
me. To my left a glass of the
vibrant West Coast IPA from
Hardywood Park in Richmond,
Virginia. Great Return had a
sticky, green nose suggestive
of the allium family, chive-like
almost, while the tropical
fruit, citrus, hop character,
and piny notes on the palate
contrasted with the sweetness
and fruitiness of the dish and
lifted it to another level.

— *Bivalves on parade* —
### MAROONED ON HOG
### ISLAND
21st Amendment
Brewery
San Francisco,
CA, USA
{ 21st-amendment.com }
OYSTER STOUT, 7.9%

Oysters and stout are one
of the great gastronomic
combinations. The next logical
step: add oysters to a stout.
True oyster stouts are rare: a
London brewery added oyster
extract to its oatmeal stout
before World War II, while a
brewery in the Isle of Man also
did something similar. In 2012,
21st Amendment came up
with this eloquent and silky
stout, which has 450 pounds
(204 kg) of oyster shells from
local Hog Island added during
the brew. And when your glass
is ready, line up six Hog Island
Sweetwater oysters.

— *The slow-cooking one* —
## MONOLITH
Burning Sky
Firle, UK
{ burningskybeer.com }
WOOD-AGED BEER, 8%

The name of this remarkable beer suggests
the mysterious object in the movie *2001: A
Space Odyssey*, or an implacable Easter Island
statue, its sightless eyes looking out over the
Pacific. The reality is much more down-to-earth.
Ultimately, this is a calm beer that has held its
own among the disorder and disorientation of
aging within a barrel that once held red wine. In
the glass, it's as dark as the soul of a demented
demagogue, although there's the potential of
redemption with the crown of crema-colored
foam. There's toffee, treacle, smoke, cherry, and
a woodiness on the nose, with a perceptible
glaze of acidity and booziness joining in.
Carbonation is soft, a prickly pepperiness says
hi, joined by a dark, wine-like headiness and
then it's vanilla, chocolate, cherries, licorice,
and a stroke of creaminess before heading
for a dry and bitter finish. Try it with beef
bourguignon or a similarly rich stew, and you
will find yourself continuing to ponder the
significance of its name.

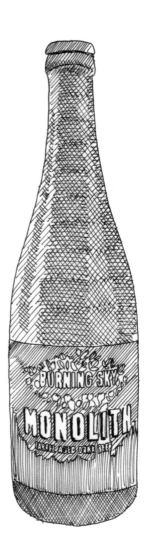

*— The Parma drama —*

### PANIL BARRIQUEÈ SOUR

Panil Birra Artigianale
— Birrificio
Torrechiara
Torrechiara, Italy
{ panilbeer.it }
FLEMISH RED, 8%

The village of Torrechiara
in northern Italy is a short
drive south of Parma, which
might give you a clue to what
you might want to eat with
this highly complex riff on a
Flemish Red. Grab a plate of
the best Parma ham you can
find, and watch how its salty-
sweet succulence bonds with
the tart, crisp, vinous, earthy,
thirst-quenching, sour-sweet
nature of a beer that has spent
its time slumbering in casks
that originally held red wine.
There is an immediate sense
of companionship.

*— Good Thai-dings —*

### ASAP

Browar Artezan
Błonie, Poland
{ artezan.pl }
DOUBLE IPA 8%

Such is the all-embracing
nature of the global beer
revolution that it isn't
surprising to learn that
Polish craft breweries are
producing Double IPAs, some
of which, like this one, are
rather enticing. Naturally, it's
a big-flavored beer, singing
with zinging hop character,
bursting with rich tropical and
citrus fruit, with a coruscating
show of bitterness and
dryness in the finish. A bold
choice for a dish is needed — a
Thai red curry. The spice and
chiles merge with the hop-
driven bitterness of the beer
to create an extra element to
the dish. West Coast America
meets central Poland meets
Thailand.

*— Duck à la cherry beers —*

### KRIEK

Cascade Brewing
Portland, OR, USA
{ cascadebrewing.com }
KRIEK, 8.1%

There's nothing ordinary
about the beers Cascade
makes at its Portland
brewpub, a light and airy
space in the Belmont district.
Kriek came about when a
red beer was being soured in
oak barrels, and brewmaster
Ron Gansberg recalls that it
seemed to cry out for oodles
of local cherries to help with
the finish. The result is a thirst-
quenching, refreshing lambic-
style beer, with cherries on the
nose and palate, balanced by
caramel maltiness and wood-
inspired vanilla and cinnamon.
When the temperature drops,
serve this with roast duck and
feel your palate soar.

— *Tapas on tap* —
## X-RAY
BrewFist
Codogno, Italy
{ new.brewfist.com }
IMPERIAL PORTER,
8.5%

———— ❦ ————

In Venice for the first time
I was told to visit Il Santo
Bevitore, a bar just off the
Strada Nova. Among the beers
from Italian craft breweries
on show, there was BrewFist's
X-Ray, a compelling Imperial
porter that was packed with
licorice, chocolate, smoke,
caramel, herbal notes, a
smooth and creamy mouthfeel,
and a long dry finish, with
plenty of dark fruit. A stand-
alone drink you might think,
but then I tried matching it
with the various tapas on
the bar — salt cod, prawns,
tuna, and dried tomato —
and much to my surprise the
beer embraced them like old
friends.

— *Chicken and demon* —
## DEMON HUNTER
Birrificio Montegioco
Val Grue, Italy
{ birrificiomontegioco.com }
STRONG BELGIAN-
STYLE ALE, 8.5%

———— ❦ ————

Demon Hunter sounds like
a ferocious beer, the kind of
beer whose name is used to
frighten those of a nervous
disposition, the kind of beer
that rocks out of the glass
with the ferocity of a dragon
in *Game of Thrones*. Don't
be deceived — the first sip
of this strong amber-hued
Belgian ale reveals a gentle
harmony of dark stone fruit
(dates, ripe plums), grape-like
sprightliness, deep caramel,
a light honeyed tone, and
a warm, mellow, alcoholic
finish. It is smooth and
civilized, complex and flexible,
and a good companion to
roasted chicken slathered with
herbs and butter.

— *Beer, mom and apple pie* —
## CONNTUCKY LIGHTNIN'
Two Roads Brewing
Stratford, CT,
USA
{ tworoadsbrewing.com }
WOOD-AGED ALE, 8.5%

———— ❦ ————

This bourbon barrel–aged
beer is brewed with a
grist including corn grits
(usually a no-no for small
breweries), which, according
to brewer Phil Markowski, is
essential to match bourbon's
characteristic sweetness, and
then sour mashed (another
bourbon characteristic),
before spending post-
fermentation time in bourbon
barrels. The result is a strong,
characterful beer dispensing
whiskey, oak, and vanilla
notes. A scoop of the same
flavored ice cream and maybe
some apple pie make the
perfect accompaniment.

— *Steak holder* —

## DARK FORCE

Haandbryggeriet
Drammen, Norway

{ haandbryggeriet.no }

IMPERIAL STOUT, 9%

This is an Imperial stout. How could it not be, with its edge-of-space darkness in the glass; its eruption of roasted grains, mocha coffee, milk chocolate, and licorice on the nose; its creamy mouthfeel — in which more mocha, chocolate, roastiness appear alongside stone fruits (plums, cherries) — and its dry, slightly boozy finish? However, there's also a crispness in the mouthfeel, while this small Norwegian brewery has designated Dark Force an Imperial Wheat Stout, with the wheat making it easy to drink. Your order: a juicy steak, but easy on the fries.

— *Finnish your pudding* —

## SAHTI OLD WORLD ALE

Aotearoa Breweries
Kawerau, New Zealand

SAHTI, 9%

Sahti is perhaps one of the world's shyest beer styles, a Finnish rural beer that was traditionally brewed with juniper berries, various cereals, few hops, and baker's yeast. According to Tammy Viitakangas at Aotearoa, this version uses manuka tips rather than juniper branches (though berries were used), while a Weissbier strain of yeast did the fermentation work. The result is a beer with a sweet banana nose, while on the palate, rye, spice, cough-drop herbiness, and more bananas make an appearance. Cherry cheesecake might be the only option.

— *Gouda go!* —

## IMPERIAL OATMEAL STOUT

Oproer Brouwerij
Utrecht, the
Netherlands

{ oproerbrouwerij.nl }

IMPERIAL STOUT, 9.5%

Oproer is a small, lively brewpub in Utrecht with the declared intention to make beers that the locals would like to drink. Hence this Imperial Oatmeal Stout, a dark, towering, potent beer with an unlikely softness. It's pitch-black in the glass and brims with chocolate, coffee, roasted grains, and a sweetness and smoothness delivered by the oats; there's even a hint of citrus halfway along the palate, plus a bitterness and dryness from the roastiness. It would be a perfect match for a nice hunk of aged Gouda.

*— Croquette power —*
## WESTMALLE TRIPEL
Brouwerij der Trappisten
van Westmalle
Westmalle, Belgium
{ trappistwestmalle.be }
**TRIPEL, 9.5%**

When we think about collaboration in the brewing world, we should not forget that Trappist beers are the original collaboration beers, an alliance forged between the sacred world of Cistercian monks and the profane one of commercial brewing. Westmalle Tripel is regarded as one of the most generously flavored and well endowed of this type. First brewed in the 1930s, it was only in the 1950s that the brewing monk Brother Thomas perfected the style. Corn gold in color, and blessed with a saintly halo of billowing snow-white foam, it has lemon, barley sugar, and sweet orange on the nose, while it is champagne-like on the palate, with rich orange, malt sweetness, and a delightful hop tingle on the finish. It's ideal with the cheese that the Westmalle monks have a hand in making — a soft, creamy, slightly salty creation that is an ideal snack with the beer; try the beer also with the delicious cheese croquettes served at the popular Café Trappisten, across the road from the abbey. Divine indeed.

SOME OF THESE BEERS ARE
BROODING, STRONG, AND
IRON-LIKE IN THEIR GRIP ON
THE PALATE; OTHERS ARE
SPECULATIVE AND SEDUCTIVE, BUT
ALL OF THEM HAVE DEEP SOULS
THAT ARE BEST APPRECIATED
WHEN SIPPED.

# CONTEMPLATIVE

# CLASSIC BEER BOOKS

## THE NOTED BREWERIES OF GREAT BRITAIN AND IRELAND
(1889)

In the late 19th century, journalist Alfred Barnard visited scores of British and Irish breweries and produced this four-volume magnum opus. It's an exceedingly rare set of volumes these days, although it is possible to find them online — there are line drawings of breweries, and descriptions of the brewing processes and the beers that he tasted (the words "brisk," "sparkling," "bright," and "vigorous" crop up a lot), plus some hammy travel writing about the towns and cities in which the breweries were based. You could argue that this was the first modern beer book.

## THE BOOK OF BEER
Andrew Campbell
(1956)

No one has ever found out who Andrew Campbell was, but whoever he was he lives on with what the author described as an attempt "to consider beer as a national beverage, and to consider it seriously." There are chapters on the brewing process, the raw materials, history, the customs of ale and beer, contemporary beers, and beer with and in food. One section is unintentionally hilarious as Campbell suggests beers that could accompany each stage of the day from breakfast onward.

## THE WORLD GUIDE TO BEER
Michael Jackson
(1977)

This was the book that kicked off Michael Jackson's lifelong career as a pioneering beer writer (or beer-hunter as he came to be known). This was the first book to take a trip around the world of beer, which included detailed examinations of the brewing nations of Germany, Belgium, what was then called Czechoslovakia, and the British

Isles, while Scandinavia, France, Oceania, Asia, and the United States also came under scrutiny. Among Jackson's many other books, his *Great Beers of Belgium* is also worth seeking out.

## HOPS AND GLORY
Pete Brown
(2010)

The final part of this British writer's "beer trilogy" (although he has since written books on pub life and culture). For his previous book, *Three Sheets to the Wind* (2006), he had traveled the world investigating various beers and drinking cultures. *Hops and Glory* was in a similar vein, although this time Brown took a barrel of IPA around the world, along the land and sea routes that 19th-century versions of the beer would have taken from Burton-on-Trent.

## WHY BEER MATTERS
Evan Rail
(2012)

The emergence of digital publishing and the Kindle has allowed writers to cover beer in a more asymmetrical way than was formerly usual. Evan Rail's book *Why Beer Matters* is perhaps one of the best examples of this approach, as it is published in digital form only; the Prague-based American followed up with *In Praise of Hangovers*, *Triplebock*, *The Brewery in the Bohemian Forest*, and *The Meanings of Craft Beer*.

## BREW BRITANNIA
Jessica Boak and Raymond Bailey
(2014)

The history of beer has received a remarkable boost since the turn of the new millennium thanks to writers such as Martyn Cornell, Ron Pattinson, and Maureen Ogle, although one of the most successful of its kind was *Brew Britannia* by Jessica Boak and Raymond Bailey. The subtitle of the book was "The Strange Rebirth of British Beer," with the authors passing from the 1960s all the way through the real ale years of the 1970s right up to the current fascination with craft beer.

188

— *Bottle of the Ardennes* —
**BELLEVAUX BLACK**
Brasserie de Bellevaux
Malmedy, Belgium
{ brasseriedebellevaux.be }
OLD ALE, 6.3%

Somewhere in the countryside
outside Malmedy, you will find
Brasserie de Bellevaux, on a
farm where former chemist Wil
Schuwer founded it in 2004.
Bellevaux Black is his memory
of the English strong ale Old
Peculier, and in the glass it is
a sleek, dark, chestnut color,
with an autumnal aroma of
berries, a smoothness on the
palate punctuated by spikes
of roast and dryness before
finishing with an appetizing
dryness. It's a beer to mull
over, to contemplate, to
think about. After all, in the
Ardennes, especially during
the winter months, you need a
glass of something to nourish
your thoughts.

— *Jaunty contemplation* —
**OND SMOKED PORTER**
Bevog Brewery
Bad Radkersburg,
Austria
{ bevog.at }
PORTER, 6.3%

Seek out your favorite armchair. By your side, a glass of
this impenetrably dark porter,
with its crema-colored head of
foam, perched atop the beer
as jaunty as an Alpine hat.
Consider the gentle yet
persistent aromatics of
roasted grain, wood smoke,
and milk chocolate
emerging from the glass, and
then plunge into its deep, rich,
and roasty character, with
accompaniments of caramel,
chocolate, smoke, and dark
fruit before the bitter and dry
finish. This is a beer to ponder
on and muse about, and most
of all to relish with the deep
contentment of the
connoisseur.

— *A Flemish masterpiece* —
**SOUR BROWN**
Thornbridge Brewery
Bakewell, UK
{ thornbridgebrewery.co.uk }
FLEMISH BROWN ALE,
7%

Sometimes it's the beer as
well as the drinker that
engages in contemplation.
And for once let us imagine a
beer as a living thing, able to
experience time and space.
What would Sour Brown, a
grand Old Master of a Flemish
brown, dream of during its two
years slumbering in Burgundy
red wine casks into which
rhubarb, Morello cherries,
and raspberries are added?
Perhaps it dreams in color
of a beer that is tart, vinous,
earthy, sour, and sweet,
fruity as in cherry, currant,
and plum-sweetness, and all
wrapped up in a cedar wood
dryness. Or perhaps that's
our dream.

— *A Greek odyssey* —
## ORA STOUT
Patraiki Brewery
Patras, Greece
{ facebook.com/patrabeer/ }
STOUT, 7%

— *Smooth, soothing sipper* —
## OLD FREDDY WALKER
Moor Beer
Bristol, UK
{ moorbeer.co.uk }
OLD ALE, 7.4%

— *Brooder of a Doppelbock* —
## SPEZIATOR
Brauhaus Riegele
Augsburg, Germany
{ riegele.de }
DOPPELBOCK, 7.5%

With this ravishing glass of dark chestnut-colored stout to hand, you might want to sit back and contemplate the nature of the Greek independent beer scene, which seems to be in a fine state of growth if ORA is any indication. This is a creamy and roasty beer in which vanilla, coffee, chocolate, a peppery hoppiness, and a slight acidity are reminiscent of what is usually found in a Foreign Export Stout. It's luscious and lubricious, glides down the throat with the ease of a landslide of flavor, and is probably best enjoyed sitting in a book-lined study reading *The Odyssey*.

Sleek and senuous-looking in the glass, this moonless sky of a beer was originally born in the middle of the Somerset countryside, but is now brewed in urban Bristol. The nose soothes with notes of licorice, mocha coffee, cocoa powder, and milk chocolate, and then the palate kicks off with a smooth and creamy milky chocolate start that is balanced by an appetizing smokiness; the finish is creamy, smooth, and dry. And Freddy? He was a former British Royal Navy submariner who lived in the village where this was first brewed, and liked nothing better than a drop of the beer that was named after him.

Augsburg-based Riegele's Doppelbock is a beer with which contemplation makes an ideal companion. The color is dark and brooding, though its crown of snow-white foam stops it from being too introspective. Then there's the nose: smooth aromatics of caramel, hazelnut, chocolate, and roast barley leap out of the glass. On the palate, the elegance continues with a light fruitiness, followed by caramel, hazelnut, chocolate, and coffee; the mouthfeel is smooth and creamy, while the finish is slightly sweet, but an appetizing dryness manages to stop it toppling into an excess of sweetness.

— *Brown. Celebrate it.* —
### IMPERIAL BROWN ALE
Nøgne ø
Grimstad, Norway
{ nogne-o.com }
BROWN ALE, 7.5%

You have to feel sorry for the color brown. It's
not regarded as the most lustrous of colors,
when you consider the fieriness and passion
that red can invoke, or the mystery of black.
When it comes to brown ale, the first things that
many will think of are the thin and sweet brown
ales of 20th-century England, especially one
in the northeast of the country. On the other
hand, thanks to US brewers, we have seen a
more vibrant and rich rendering of brown ale,
of which this Imperial version is a fine example.
Both the nose and palate pulsate with caramel,
mocha coffee, hazelnuts, and roast malt, in
conjunction with a rich and bittersweet
mouthfeel. Brown is the new black indeed.

— *Thoughtful* —
### CAPE OF GOOD HOPS
Cape Brewing Company
Paarl, South Africa
{ capebrewing.co.za }
IMPERIAL IPA, 7.5%

Consider the moment on first meeting a beer.
What to do? The playful drinker might grasp the
glass and attack with relish and lip-smacking
gusto, without pausing to contemplate the
color and the aromas. Others, perhaps more
thoughtful, will take their time, gauge the color.
If face to face with Cape of Good Hops, notice
first its dark golden gleam, held like a caged
dragon, beneath a creamy white head of foam.
Next, the aromatics: a deep fruitiness, and a
pine-charged resinousness. Finally, the taste:
citrus, tropical fruit stationed on a bittersweet
platform of malt before a dry finish. What to
do next? Contemplate another sip. And then
another.

*— Hush in the hustle —*
**SUPER BITTER**
Birrificio Baladin
Piozzo, Italy
{ birreria.com }
BELGIAN-STYLE STRONG ALE, 8%

Amid the bustle and boisterousness of a small
indoor market in Bologna, I grabbed a glass of
Super Bitter from Le Baladin bar and was
immediately deep in contemplation in its
company. It's 8%, and for that reason alone
it's pretty far away from the usual concept
of a bitter. It's also a beer to be drunk with
thoughtfulness. Dark orange in color, with a
deep orange fruitiness (marmalade perhaps),
it's chewy and spicy, with almond, and more
orange as well as a bittersweet rustle in
the finish. And as I drank it, the activities in
the market revolving around me, I was too
engrossed in the beer to notice anything.

*— A light in the darkness —*
**SIGTUNA MIDVINTERBLOT**
Sigtuna Brygghus
Stockholm, Sweden
{ sigtunabrygghus.se }
IMPERIAL PORTER, 8%

Long, dark winters are a feature of
Scandinavian life, which is why festivals such
as the old Viking-inspired Midvinterblot throw
a bit of light onto the gloom. Sigtuna's lush
Imperial porter is another instance of luminos-
ity that can make this period of darkness a lot
more tolerable. All you have to do is find a quiet
corner and pour this dark chestnut-brown beer
into a glass, then first of all inhale the coffee,
demerara sugar, toffee, roasted barley, and milk
chocolate notes, a warm and smooth embrace
that then leads into more of the same on the
palate alongside a creamy mouthfeel and a
long, lingering, bittersweet finish. Winter nights
are made for this kind of beer.

*— Wooden it be nice —*

## OLA DUBH

Harviestoun
Alva, UK
{ harviestoun.com }
**WOOD-AGED ALE, 8%**

So this is what happens. Harviestoun's
magnificently rich porter Old Engine Oil is
brewed to a gigantic 10.5%, and then aged
in oak barrels that once provided a home to
various vintages of Highland Park's Single Malt
Whisky. There are three different expressions
available: Ola Dubh 12, 16, and 18. Let's look at
the last named, which is a great example of how
we can stretch what beer can do: it is dark and
deep in color, and still and limpid in the glass.
On the nose flurries of coffee, chocolate, and
tobacco join in with traces of vanilla in the background; the palate is busy with a chocolate and
mocha character, though stern iodine notes in
the mid-palate stop the beer from going too far
toward Starbucks. There is a creaminess and a
soothing hand on the brow in the mouthfeel in
the way it glides over the palate. The finish has
a hint of stern smokiness in the finish, although
a chime of bittersweetness stops it from
becoming too overwhelming.

*— Thank Santa —*

## CORSENDONK CHRISTMAS ALE

Brouwerij Corsendonk
(brewed at Brasserie du
Bocq)
Turnhout, Belgium
BELGIAN STRONG ALE,
8.1%

Christmas is the ideal time for contemplation, and a beer for this time of the season needs to be strong and rich in its flavors. Here is one such libation. Allowed out of the bottle, it's a dark chestnut-brown, with crimson tints as if reflecting the warming Yuletide fire. Rich, rousing wafts of caramel, chocolate, and spice declare themselves in the aromas, while to sip it is to experience a swoon of chocolate, ripe plums, Christmas spice, and cherry-like sweetness, alongside a creamy mouthfeel.

*— Canalside contemplater —*

## DUITS & LAURET WINTERSTOUT

Speciaalbierbrouwerij
Duits & Lauret
Everdingen, the
Netherlands
{ duitslauret.com }
STOUT, 8.5%

I was in a bar opposite a canal in Amsterdam one winter's evening. Rain was lashing down outside, but all I cared about was this incredibly silky and sinuous stout, which was implacable in its darkness in the glass. It was a fascinating beer, holding all my attention, a lit fuse of chocolate, mocha, raisins, and orange fizzing away on the nose, before the same flavors exploded on the palate. It had depth and mystery, and was the perfect companion for this cold and wet night of contemplation and speculation.

*— A flutter of wings —*

## BACK IN BLACK

Naparbier
Noáin, Navarre, Spain
{ naparbier.com }
BLACK IPA, 8.5%

Sometimes you need to keep an eye on your beer to see what is left. With this remarkable Black IPA — its heart as dark as the stories of H. P. Lovecraft — as the beer is drunk, the lacework of foam, whorls, and curls left on the inside of the glass is a work of art as it lingers, a remembrance of the beer. Just like the foam, the memory of Back In Black remains, with its intense level of dryness, an ululation of roastiness, a flutter of deep orange pungency, the smoothness of licorice, all jamming together to create a beer that is complete in its contemplation.

CONTEMPLATIVE

SEVEN MOODS OF CRAFT BEER

*— Fearless —*

## SPAGHETTI WESTERN

BrewFist

Codogno, Italy

{ newbrewfist.com }

**IMPERIAL STOUT, 8.7%**

BrewFist was part of the second wave of the
Italian craft beer revolution, an outfit that
looked to hops to provide the buzz, a group
who weren't afraid to look at US craft brewers
and think that they would like some of that
lupulin-love and general craziness. One of the
results was this muscular, eye-popping Imperial
stout, the result of a journey and collaboration
that saw BrewFist cross the Atlantic to
Oklahoma to work with Prairie Artisan Ales.
It is a richly flavored beer, with the addition
of coffee and cocoa nibs adding depth and
complexity. As the alcohol strength suggests,
this is a beer to be respected, though its smooth
mouthfeel makes it dangerously drinkable,
which is why you need a comfortable armchair
for it. To spice things up, some expressions of
this beer have been available after being aged
in grappa barrels. There is definitely no fear in
the way BrewFist approaches its beers.

> "IT WAS OF THE MOST
> BEAUTIFUL COLOR
> THAT THE EYE OF
> AN ARTIST IN BEER
> COULD DESIRE."
> THOMAS HARDY, *THE
> TRUMPET-MAJOR,* 1880

— *Crossing continents* —

**BALTIC PORTER**

Redoak Brewery

Sydney, Australia

{ redoak.com.au }

BALTIC PORTER, 9%

It's a long way from Eastern Europe to Australia, but this dark, ruby-colored beer is a link between the two worlds. This is a Baltic porter, a style of beer that was once popular around the eponymous region, but then fell off in popularity as golden lagers rolled across the area with the persistence of an invading horde. It has slowly re-emerged in its home region, but in the meantime, it was left to the likes of Redoak to rediscover and redefine this beer, with its rich chocolate and mocha coffee notes on the nose and palate, allied with a smooth malt character, and a warming and bittersweet finish.

— *London calling* —

**IMPERIAL BROWN STOUT**

The Kernel Brewery

London, UK

{ thekernelbrewery.com }

IMPERIAL STOUT, 9%

(ABV VARIES)

This is a journey back in time to London in 1856, when this beer was first brewed. Naturally, due to different brewing techniques and raw materials, it won't taste exactly the same as it did then, but we do have a chance to imagine the taste of the 19th century. There's a dark chocolate sweetness on the nose, soothing with a background of vanilla. In the glass, it has the creaminess of chocolate-covered nuts, a mid-palate sweetness, a hint of coconut, and a bitterness and fullness that leave a delicious impression.

— *Poirot in a pint* —

**HERCULE STOUT**

Ellezelloise (Brasserie des Légendes)

Ellezelles, Belgium

{ www.brasseriedeslegendes.be }

IMPERIAL STOUT, 9%

The famous fictional detective Hercule Poirot appears on the label of this beer for good reason: he was born in Ellezelles. This rich and creamy self-styled "Belgian stout" is perfect for contemplating the creation of one of crime fiction's greatest detectives. In the glass, the beer is as dark as a murderer's motive, a silent, inscrutable motive that hides beneath a rocky crema-colored head of foam. It is chewy and creamy, full-bodied, low in its roastiness (mocha rather than espresso in its coffee note), and dashed with a plummy fruitiness before finishing with a swirl of dryness.

*— Like a monk —*
## BEDE'S CHALICE
Durham Brewery
Durham, UK
{ durhambrewery.com }
TRIPEL, 9%

Did the Venerable Bede, whose remains now lie in Durham Cathedral, like a drop of ale? Given the propensity of monks for conviviality, when they weren't on their knees, he might have, and this bright golden Belgian-style Tripel could have been just the beer to aid him in his prayers and contemplation. It's an intriguing interpretation of a Tripel, full and lubricious, with a brittle, crystalline citrusiness on the nose alongside a murmur of caramel sweetness. There's a Cointreau-like fieriness on the palate along with white pepper and more caramel before it finishes dry and spirituous. A beer that is at once serious and jolly, just like a monk.

*— From Perth with love —*
## BORIS
Feral Brewing
Perth, Australia
{ feralbrewing.com.au }
IMPERIAL STOUT, 9.1%

This is a beer style of historical importance, a link with the dark, strong ales that were sent to the Russian Empire in the late 18th century and favored by Catherine the Great. It's a long way in space, time, and temperature from Perth, Australia, to the Baltic, but Feral's Imperial stout is a classic of its style, brimming with deep chocolate and coffee, roasted barley, dark ripe fruits, and a confidence in its own ability to make its drinker stop and ponder the mystery of beer. It's also a peerless winter warmer, even in Perth, whose winters are mild, though when it rains, as it does a lot during this season, this is the beer to get you through it.

— *Pacific* —
## TROUBADOUR WESTKUST
Brouwerij The Musketeers (brewed
at De Proefbrouwerij)
Ursel, Belgium
{ troubadourbeers.com }
**BLACK IPA, 9.2%**

Why have a brewery when you can create your
beers at another one? That's the question The
Musketeers (who are actually four, just like in
Dumas' novel) asked themselves when they
considered their brewing options — thankfully
De Proefbrouwerij stepped into the breach. The
arrangement has certainly worked, especially
when we consider Westkust (West Coast in
Flemish), a particularly powerful black IPA
brimming with milk chocolate, mocha coffee,
grapefruit, lightly roasted malt, and the kind
of bittersweet finish that lingers long in the
memory. It's a beer of lasting potency, a
brooding, serious beer.

— *A soulful survivor* —
## ZYWEIC PORTER
Grupa Zyweic
Zyweic, Poland
{ zywiec.com.pl }
**BALTIC PORTER, 9.5%**

This might be a beer conceived in the latter
part of the 19th century, but its survival is a
matter for celebration and consumption. It
one of the few surviving original Baltic porters,
a beer style whose origins are in the strong
dark beers once exported from the UK to the
Russian Empire. Now it's under another empire,
that of Heineken-owned Zyweic, but it's not
been dumbed down or devastated by this
change. In the glass, it's the kind of darkness
that is all-enveloping, while chocolate, mocha
coffee, roast barley, and a vinous note all crave
attention on the nose and palate, before its
bitter, dry, roasty finish. This is a survivor that
demands to be brought to every contemplative
drinker's attention.

198

*— The beast outside —*
### BIGFOOT
Sierra Nevada
Chico, CA, USA
{ sierranevada.com }
BARLEY WINE, 9.6%
(ABV CHANGES ANNUALLY)

Bigfoot is the right name for this monstrous beast of a barley wine that Sierra Nevada has produced annually since 1983. It's bold, it's boisterous, it rouses the senses and intensifies the pleasure that sometimes only a big barley wine can bring. Its alcoholic strength changes from year to year, and some like to leave it for several years before drinking it, mad about the mellowness that time can bring. Reddish-brown in color, it has an intense denseness of fruitiness on the nose, accompanied by toffee and pine-like notes from the hops. It's a full-bodied—chewy even—beer in the mouthfeel, warming from all the alcohol (when it was first brewed, it was the strongest beer in the United States), plunging the palate into a deep fruiti-ness (orange marmalade), alongside a sweet-ness reminiscent of demerara sugar, caramel, and a long, bitter finish that lasts and lasts. Contemplation, consecration, consideration — this is a beer that you can write and think about all night long.

*— A wedding beer —*
## HARD BRIDE
AleBrowar (brewed at
Browar Gościszewo)
Lebork, Poland
{ alebrowar.pl }
**BARLEY WINE, 9.8%**

——— ❧ ———

This beer was brewed for the
marriage of brewer Michał,
and, according to his colleague Bartek, "the guests
were so delighted that it
became a regular beer." It must
have been some wedding,
given the 9.8% strength. It's an
American-style barley wine,
dark amber in color, with
pine resin, ripe orange, and
whispers of tropical fruit and
caramel on the nose; sipped
slowly, it reveals more citrus
and tropical fruit, caramel,
and pine, alongside a full body
and an enticing smoothness.
The finish is bittersweet, with
a flush of alcohol. Drink at
ease and repent at leisure.

*— Darkness visible —*
## WILD THING
Murray's
Port Stephens, NSW,
Australia
{ murraysbrewingco.com.au }
**IMPERIAL STOUT, 10%**

——— ❧ ———

Come the winter months,
Murray's takes its fans into the
comfort zone of a big and
bullish Imperial stout
(incidentally one of the first
Australian craft brewery riffs
on the style). The color is as
dark as deep space; there's
an equally uncompromising
character to both its taste and
aroma: mocha coffee beans,
chocolate, roasted grains,
and licorice are all daubed on
this potent alcoholic canvas.
The brewery obviously likes
to have fun with this beer:
another beer, Wild Thing
Chocolate, sees bitter dark
cocoa nibs and vanilla pods
being added.

*— A Bavarian aria —*
## IMPERIAL STOUT
Private Landbrauerei
Schönram
Petting, Germany
{ brauerei-schoenram.de }
**IMPERIAL STOUT, 10%**

——— ❧ ———

It had been a busy day in
Berlin, and I was due a restful
evening in Meisterstuck, a
cool and moody restaurant.
A glass of Pils was devoured,
and then I wanted something
relaxing. Along came a glass of
this Imperial stout, the first I'd
had from a Bavarian brewery.
It was a deep Burgundy red
in color, and from the glass
swirled aromas of molasses,
marzipan, coffee liqueur, and
vanilla. I drank and found
myself in a deep forested
valley of mocha, cocoa,
bittersweetness, big alcohol,
woodiness, and yet more
vanilla. The day's travails
vanished like smoke.

— *Dark side of De Molen* —

## DE MOLEN HEL & VERDOEMENIS

Brouwerij de Molen
Bodegraven, the
Netherlands

{ brouwerijdemolen.nl }

IMPERIAL STOUT, 10%

A wide range of styles and beers are produced at De Molen — up to 20 on a regular basis; something new is brewed every four weeks or so; and there's a lot of barrel aging. With all this activity, Hel & Verdoemenis is probably the ideal beer with which to calm things down. An American version of Imperial stout, it focuses on the bitter, roasty, coffee-like side of the style, while bringing in chocolate, some hop character (herbal and floral notes), and a sense of overwhelming complexity. Naturally enough, there are barrel-aged versions of this.

— *The long road* —

## RIDGEWAY IMPERIAL BARLEY WINE

Ridgeway Brewery
South Stoke, UK

{ ridgewaybrewery.co.uk }

BARLEY WINE, 10%

This bruiser of a barley wine gleams burnished gold in the glass, while tiny bubbles effortlessly float to the top. It's a complex-tasting beer, with caramel, pepper, spice, hops, and a candied sweetness on both the nose and the palate; the dry finish follows a sweet golden syrup-like character, with added bitterness and a fiery alcoholic kick. This is a beer to be treated with respect. Ridgeway brews its beers in rural Oxfordshire, not far from the ancient track that gives it its name, while the brewery's founder was once head brewer at the famous Brakspear's in Henley.

— *Fathomless* —

## BELOW DECKS

Heavy Seas
Baltimore, MD, USA

{ hsbeer.com }

BARLEY WINE, 10%

Barley wine is the ultimate contemplative beer: a strong, potent, deep-souled, and meditative drink. Below Decks, which is aged for 12 months in red wine barrels, enchants on first pour with its flurry of dried fruit and vinous hints on the nose. For the taste, which rocks around the mouth like a galleon in a swell, imagine sherry, the tannins of red wine, ripe plum, vanilla, the ghost of cherries, malt sweetness, dark malts, and a bittersweet finish. Brewed every year, this is part of the brewery's "Uncharted Waters" beer series, which has also included a gingerbread Weizenbock aged in rum barrels.

— *The old ales of Germany* —

## ADAM

Hair of the Dog
Portland, OR, USA
{ hairofthedog.com }
ADAMBIER, 10%

Portland is perhaps one of the best cities in the United States, if not the world, in which to drink beer, and every pilgrim who visits there is recommended to wend their way to Hair of the Dog's tasting rooms, where the beers are also brewed. In this light and airy space on a corner in the Belmont district (an area itself home to many good taprooms), the brewery's range of European-influenced beers can be examined and studied, with the powerful and potent Adam usually being experienced at the conclusion of such research. Brewed with an ancient German beer style, Adambier, in mind, it is a beast of a beer with notes of chocolate, toffee, smoke, dark fruits such as ripe plum, pepper, old books, leather, and a quinine-like spike of bitterness all working together to produce an incredibly complex and thoughtful beer. With this strength and the kaleidoscopic range of flavors and aromas, Adam is also a beer to be laid down for a future evening when, far away from Hair of the Dog's tasting rooms, you can toast time well spent in Portland.

— *Let the snow fall* —
## THE VERMONSTER
Rock Art Brewery
Morrisville, VT, USA
{ rockartbrewery.com }
**BARLEY WINE, 10%**

I once met Rock Art's founder, Matt Nadeau, when traveling through Vermont and, among other things, we discussed the heavy snowfall that happens most winters in the brewery's vicinity. He conjured up images of snowbound villages, biting northerlies, and, most importantly, cozy log fires in front of which a glass of this behemoth of a barley wine would be ideal to accompany your contemplation of the harshness of a Vermont winter. This is the kind of beer that you need time to study: it's dark amber in color, and has rich elements of caramel, roast grains, hazelnut, and citrus all creating their own pathway to paradise. The finish is bitter, citrusy, and dry, and all you need now is for the snow to come.

— *An elegant, complex companion* —
## TEN FIDY
Oskar Blues
Longmont, CO, USA
{ oskarblues.com }
**IMPERIAL STOUT, 10.5%**

Seeing is not always believing; especially when I was first given Ten Fidy to drink. It was in a can, at a time when craft beers in cans were a novelty, and those that did find their way into them were usually pale ales rather than this big, bellowing, Imperial stout. It was strange to see the midnight-black color of the beer coming out of the can but, once I'd got over that, there was a beautiful Imperial stout to savor, with chocolate, coffee, vanilla, licorice, and roast grain on both the nose and the palate. For many it was the start of the "craft can" revolution but, container aside, it's the elegance and complexity of this beer that make it memorable.

— *Contemplate Brazilian* —

## COLORADO ITHICA

Cervejaria Colorado
Ribeirão Preto, Brazil
{ cervejariacolorado.com.br }
IMPERIAL STOUT,
10.5%

❧

In 2015, the Brazilian craft
brewery Cervejaria Colorado
was acquired by AB InBev.
Despite this change in owner-
ship, the beers are still brewed
to their old high standards:
beers such as Colorado Ithaca
(or Vintage Black Rapadura
as it is known in the United
States), a lush Imperial stout
that mixes American craft
ambience (it's well hopped, for
a start) with the brewery's own
take on things — rapadura
sugar is added. The result is
a restful and complex beer in
which berry fruit, toffee, milky
coffee, a creamy mouthfeel,
and an assertive bitter
finish all play their life-
affirming part.

— *Northern comfort* —

## JÚDAS NR. 16
## QUADRUPLE

Borg Brugghús
Reykjavík, Iceland
{ borgbrugghus.is }
BELGIAN-STYLE
QUADRUPLE, 10.5%

❧

Borg Brugghús is a small outfit
owned by Egill Skallagríms-
son, one of the biggest
breweries in Iceland. Their
beers are uniformly good,
but especially Júdas Nr. 16
Quadruple. Soft zephyrs of
milk chocolate drift across the
nose on first pass, but then
there is the sternness of a rye
cracker or even Marmite, plus
a vinous note that's suggestive
of an old wine barrel. It is fiery
and fruity on the palate, with
nougat, cherry brandy,
woodiness, toasted
marshmallows, sugared cold
coffee, and a juicy full
mouthfeel. A remarkable beer
from the far north.

— *Knowledge through noise* —

## CLOUT STOUT

Nail Brewing
Bassendean, Australia
{ nailbrewing.com.au }
IMPERIAL STOUT,
10.6%
(ABV VARIES)

❧

Once a year, Clout Stout is
released, an Imperial stout, a
deep and unctuous beer that
pulsates with the rhythms
of dark and roast malts. It's
a limited edition, and not
cheap. It's a muscular beer, an
intense drinking
experience, a beer upon which
to reflect as it sits brooding in
the glass, its array of
aromatics including caramel-
flecked and dark fruit
sweetness, the soothing
stroke of vanilla, and the bite
of roast grain. The mouthfeel
is creamy, almost oily, and the
big, bittersweet, and dry finish
resonates like the echo of
applause in a concert hall.

— *Past, present, and future* —
### THE CZAR
Avery
Boulder, CO, USA
{ averybrewing.com }
IMPERIAL STOUT, 10.6%
(ABV VARIES)

Deep into the night the Czar sits in contemplation, silent, summing up past, present, and
future; outside against a night sky that stretches
on toward infinity, the stars twinkle, their presence a counterweight to the brooding monolith
of the Czar. In the glass, this imperious Imperial
stout is poured, stygian in its darkness, but the
mood of introspection is broken by the sweetly
spoken aromas of toffee, mocha, chocolate,
and figs that reach out, while a sip brings forth
the same, alongside molasses, vanilla, nuts,
and a dry, slightly roast finish. Brewed annually,
this is one of Avery's star beers, which can be
enjoyed in the present or kept, like a Czar in a
jail, for the future.

— *Monstrous* —
### QUINTACERATOPS
Brooklyn Brewery
New York, NY, USA
{ brooklynbrewery.com }
BELGIAN-STYLE QUADRUPLE, 10.9%

The sleep of reason might bring forth monsters,
but the sleep that Quintaceratops' weaker
quadruple cousin, Quadraceratops, undergoes
in a set of Trinidadian rum barrels, followed by
US bourbon ones, brings forth a monstrously
resolute and even more powerful beer. The
time spent in rum barrels is suggestive of
brown sugar and spice as well as ripe currants
in the background; meanwhile the condition is
sprightly and springy, and the palate is subject
to an intense barrage of flavors, including an
earthiness suggestive of wet stone, tobacco,
demerara sugar, toffee, more rum, and Bourbon
vanilla, and a just discernable edge of palate
sourness that gives the beer its final edge. As
well as contemplation, this is a beer that will
encourage discussion.

— *Dark and dominant* —
## RHETORIC EDITION 4.1
Hardknott
Millom, UK
{ hardknott.com }
IMPERIAL STOUT, 11%

— *The power of prayer* —
## LA TRAPPE QUADRUPEL OAK AGED
Bierbrouwerij De
Koningshoeven
Berkel-Enschot, the
Netherlands
{ latrappetrappist.com }
WOOD-AGED ALE, 11%

La Trappe's Quadrupel is a beer to ponder over, a honeyed, bittersweet, and warming beer. However, its character blooms after being oak-aged (each batch is released quarterly). A gleaming amber-brown in color, its aromas and flavors will depend on the barrels from which it has been blended — as well as new oak, the beer will have spent time in other wooden barrels including those that have held port, wine, or brandy. There will be a slinky sense of vanilla, ripe dark fruit, honeyed hazelnuts, and dry grain.

Any part of the day can be brightened by a glass of this Leviathan-like Imperial stout, but it's a much more eager companion when the temperature drops and light leaks away. Produced at the end of 2015 to celebrate the 10th anniversary of this perky brewery in the Lake District, it is as dark as a hanging judge's cap, and as deep as the Earth's core, with vanilla, soot, chocolate, mocha, citrus sweetness, and roast dryness leaping out of the glass onto the nose and palate. It was also a labor of love for brewery founder Dave Bailey: the grist includes peat-smoked malt, a bag of which was delivered uncrushed. The brewery doesn't have a mill, and Bailey spent two days hand rolling the malt…

> " 'WHAT DO YOU THINK
> THE BRAVEST DRINK
> UNDER THE SKY?' 'STRONG
> BEER,' SAID I."
> ROBERT GRAVES, *STRONG BEER*, 1918

— *A Celtic contemplative* —
### XI.I SAMHAIN
Brasserie Lancelot
Le Roc Saint Andre, France
{ brasserie-lancelot.bzh }
BARLEY WINE, 11.1%

Samhain is the Celtic festival taking place over October 31 and November 1, and Lancelot, who are proud of their Breton roots, always brew this seasonal stormer at that time, so it's ready to be drunk by the turn of the winter solstice in December. Dark chestnut in color, there's a swirl of vanilla, dark chocolate, mocha, and booziness emerging from the glass: warming, comfortable, and relaxing. There's a flurry of chocolate, vanilla, mocha, fruitcake, and sambuca-like notes on the palate, a creamy mouthfeel, while the finish — dry, mellowed sweetness, and spirituous fieriness — stays with the pleasure of a remembered kiss. One to age for a future Samhain.

— *Meant for musing* —
### 10TH SANCTUM BARLEYWINE
Brickway Brewery & Distillery
Omaha, NE, USA
{ drinkbrickway.com }
BARLEY WINE, 11.2%
(ABV VARIES)

Each year, this Omaha-based brewery and distillery makes a stupendous pensive-looking barley wine, which gleams dark cherry red in the glass, a muse for deliberating on the mysterious beer style that is barley wine. It's a big, beefy, muscular, robust kind of beer, pulsating with vanilla, caramel, ripe plums, and even orange liqueur on the nose. Its alcoholic strength varies from year to year, but it is not fainthearted when it comes to taste: there is more vanilla, dark fruits, cherry, toffee, some spice, and, above all, the lift of the alcohol, which is exceptionally well integrated. As it sits there in your snifter, you will soon know that after just one taste this is a beer you want to reflect on.

— *Imperious and imperial* —
## BLACK BLOCK
Cervesa la Pirata
Súria, Spain
{ cervesalapirata.com }
IMPERIAL STOUT, 11.2%

— *Let us be led astray* —
## AUPA TOVARISCH
Laugar Brewery
Gordexola, Spain
{ www.laugarbrewery.com }
IMPERIAL STOUT, 11.3%

Brewing an Imperial stout is a challenge to smaller brewers, especially when, like La Pirata, there is no tradition of it in their home country. The brewers might have tried it on their travels, but those new to it will wonder what they have in their glass. However, if they take their time and engage in a serious study of Black Block, they will discover an imperious Imperial stout, the color of infernal night in the glass, lustrous chocolate, coffee, vanilla, and roastiness on the nose, and an unctuous, creamy, burly beer on the palate, with more chocolate and coffee, caramel, roastiness, integrated alcohol and cocoa, all wrapped up with a bitter, dry finish.

Sometimes we are led astray by our thoughts. A passage in a great novel might have us believe we are ensconced in a Dublin pub in the 1900s, waiting to attend a funeral, or lying on a forest floor prior to ambushing an armed column. Beer may have a similar effect. Take a sip of Aupa Tovarisch — the color of a well-weathered, deep mahogany sideboard inherited from an ancient aunt, its aroma and taste a hymnal of chocolate, vanilla, fudge-like sweetness, caramel, licorice, roast, and bitterness cramming the senses in the way that piety fills out a particularly devout cathedral — and you will be there, in the glass, in the taste, in the aromatics, at one with a magnificent beer.

*— A Dutch masterpiece —*
### VAN MOLL
Zoltan Highland Park
Eindhoven, the Netherlands
{ vanmolleindhoven.nl }
IMPERIAL STOUT, 12%

Eindhoven is the home to this small brewpub, which loves to experiment with its beers. Saisons are made with mint and mango, a Berliner Weisse is married with rhubarb, raspberries, and lime, while this beer sees its Imperial stout Zoltan spending six months in a Highland Park whiskey barrel. I was at a beer launch in a bar in the Dutch city of 's-Hertogenbosch when the brewery owner offered me a glass of this imperious beer. It was smoky, charry, and woody on the nose, while each sip revealed a complexity of vanilla, licorice, chocolate, and milky mocha coffee, all integrated with a bittersweet, smooth, and creamy mouthfeel. This is a Dutch masterpiece.

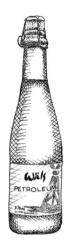

*— Time is, time was —*
### WÄLS PETROLEUM
Cervejaria Wäls
Belo Horizonte, Brazil
{ wals.com.br }
IMPERIAL STOUT, 12%

Even though Brazil is famous for the frenetic pace of its carnival lifestyle, there's always time to slow things down and let life flow by, which is when this velvety Imperial stout comes into play. Dark chestnut in color, it has a sweet nose reminiscent of Yorkshire Parkin (especially with the hint of ginger), treacle toffee, and a hop-influenced pungency. Sweet and mocha-like on the palate, with a citrusy fruitiness in the background, it is accompanied by a distinctive dryness and bitterness on the palate with a powerful alcoholic fieriness before descending to a dry finish. It was first brewed in 2010, and Brazilian beer lovers had seen nothing like it before.

**MALHEUR DARK BRUT**

Brouwerij Malheur

Buggenhout, Belgium

{ malheur.be }

**BELGIAN-STYLE STRONG ALE, 12%**

First of all there was Malheur's Bière Brut, a sprightly and sparkling blond beer that was designated as a "champagne beer," thanks partly to the method of production (involving the *dégorgement* process used in champagne-making). Ironically enough, at about the same time, another brewery in the same town came up with a champagne-style beer; maybe this was the spur to the brewery developing Dark Brut, an elegant and luxurious dark "champagne beer," which is also matured in young oak barrels that have been especially charred for it. The result is an incredibly complex and creative beer, a beer that inspires contemplation, restfulness, and even thoughts of love as it sparkles in the glass, a gleaming chestnut-brown in color. There are aromatics of sherry and even port, chocolate, spice, and vanilla. This is a beer to take your time over, as all thoughts of jobs to be done, people to be seen, books to be read, are led astray by its sensuous nature. It's delicately sweet on the palate, encouraged by a brush of more sherry, chocolate, blueberries, vanilla, and a sparkle in the mouthfeel. Take your time with this.

210

— *Fast yet slow* —

### SPEEDWAY STOUT
Alesmith Brewing
San Diego, CA, USA
{ alesmith.com }
IMPERIAL STOUT, 12%

You cannot help but think of your own mortality
in the Pine Box in Seattle. One of the city's most
acclaimed and liveliest craft beer bars,
it was also once the funeral home where Bruce
Lee was laid to rest. I was very conscious of the
history as I sat at the bar and drank a glass of
Speedway Stout, the first part of whose name
seemed at variance with the bar's previous use.
On the other hand, its somber darkness-visible
hue, and rage against the light of chocolate,
coffee, roast grains, and bitterness seemed
an appropriate drink to contemplate one's
fragile existence on this sphere spinning
through space.

— *Night falls; pour this* —

### THE ABYSS
Deschutes Brewery
Bend, OR, USA
{ deschutesbrewery.com }
IMPERIAL STOUT, 12.2%

This annually produced barrel-aged Imperial
stout is as deep in its depth of dark color and
flavor as the mines of Moria in *The Lord of the
Rings*, suggestive of a place into which you can
fall with the ease of a supplicant. There are
bourbon barrel–influenced aromatics
suggestive of vanilla, fudge, chocolate, plus
Brazilian coffee; it is sweet and woody, smooth
and mellow, spirituous and sensual. These
aromatics transfer to the flavors that coat and
arouse the palate, alongside a smooth mouthfeel and a creaminess. It's a potent cocktail of
strength and silkiness, a beer for the end of
the night, in which one can contemplate the
end of the world, and look forward to the
renewal of the dawn.

*— The snow leopard —*

**LERVIG BARLEY WINE**

Lervig Aktiebryggeri
Stavanger, Norway
{ lervig.no }
BARLEY WINE, 12.5%

Barley wines are rare beasts, fantastic animals even, the kind of beasts about which legends grow, like the snow leopard glimpsed amid the Himalayan heights. Lervig's barley wine is a snow leopard of sorts, an American-style barley wine that has spent time hiding in bourbon barrels before being glimpsed. This is a beer to savor and spend time over, if only to discover its layers of flavors and aromas, including ripe dark fruit, toffee, coconut, and vanilla, alongside the integrated blast of alcohol. You have to be lucky though: only 4,000 liters (1,056 US gallons) are brewed each year.

*— Monarchical —*

**DE STRUISE BLACK ALBERT**

De Struise Brouwers
Oostvleteren, Belgium
{ struise.com }
IMPERIAL STOUT, 13%

At 13%, this deeply flavored Imperial stout is not a beer to be trifled with. It's a sipping beer, a silent, contemplative beer that demands respect and a period of relaxation with perhaps a favorite book or piece of music (Beethoven's String Quartet No. 13 perhaps). Named after the Belgian King Albert II, it's as dark as the most moonless of nights, with a complex array of aromas, including milk chocolate, treacle, and mocha coffee. Similarly dark moments occur on the palate alongside a creamy mouthfeel, lightly roasted coffee beans, and a smooth, unctuous finish. This was originally commissioned by the owners of Ebenezer's Pub in Lovell, Maine, a bar that specializes in classic Belgian beers (like this one).

CONTEMPLATIVE

SEVEN MOODS OF CRAFT BEER

"THE WORLD ALWAYS KNEW THAT BEER WAS A NOBLE AND COMPLEX DRINK, BUT, FOR A MOMENT IN HISTORY, THAT WAS FORGOTTEN. NOW IT IS BEING REMEMBERED."
MICHAEL JACKSON, 1988

*— Winter is coming —*
## B-BOMB
Fremont Brewing
Seattle, WA, USA
{ fremontbrewing.com }
WOOD-AGED ALE, 14%

This is a beer that carves out a calmness in the eye of the storm of winter, especially when its home city of Seattle settles down resigned beneath its regular canopy of rain. Annually released every November, B-Bomb is also a harmonious marriage of barrels that once held bourbon along with a beer whose strength could hold up the Pillars of Hercules. This is the kind of beer that you take in a deep breath of before each sip of a beautifully balanced, handsomely etched, quietly assertive assemblage of bourbon, vanilla, coffee, and chocolate alongside its deep, deep, unfathomable sense of stillness and contemplation.

*— Growing older gracefully —*
## WORLD WIDE STOUT
Dogfish Head
Milton, DE, USA
{ dogfish.com }
IMPERIAL STOUT, 15-20%

Time is an added ingredient when it comes to contemplating this monstrous behemoth of any imperial stout, whose alcoholic strength grooves and moves with each year's expression. Time? Brewery founder Sam Calagione always recommends that supplicants of its intensity buy two bottles, one to slowly savor as the night draws in and thoughts meander through the day's actions. The other bottle? He suggests that it be aged, for several years, where its rich roasty vibrancy and authoritative catch of chocolate, molasses, treacle, and coffee notes deepen and mellow into a port-like persuasiveness that will make contemplation of its exclusiveness all the better.

# INDEX

215

SEVEN MOODS OF CRAFT BEER          INDEX

SEVEN MOODS OF CRAFT BEER    INDEX

# INDEX

INDEX

SEVEN MOODS OF CRAFT BEER